Weimar Cinema, Embodiment, and Historicity

T0383583

"This book recovers Ernst Lubitsch's important early historical films and shows how they provide insights into the ways in which cinematic experience has shaped historical experience to this day."

—*Todd Herzog, University of Cincinnati*

In its retrieval and (re)construction, the past has become interwoven with the images and structure of cinema. Not only have mass media—especially film and television—shaped the content of memories and histories, but they have also shaped their very form. Combining historicization with close readings of German director Ernst Lubitsch's historical films, this book focuses on an early turning point in this development, exploring how the medium of film shaped modern historical experience and understanding—how it moved embodied audiences through moving images.

Mason Kamana Allred is a historian and volume editor at the Joseph Smith Papers. His interdisciplinary work on film and media history has appeared in *The Journal of the American Academy of Religion*, *Jewish Studies Quarterly*, and *The Journal of Popular Culture* as well as the edited collections *Dorian: A Peculiar Edition* and *Film and History*.

Routledge Focus on Film Studies

1. Robot Ecology and the Science Fiction Film
J. P. Telotte

2. Weimar Cinema, Embodiment, and Historicity
Cultural Memory and the Historical Films of Ernst Lubitsch
Mason Kamana Allred

Weimar Cinema, Embodiment, and Historicity

Cultural Memory and the Historical
Films of Ernst Lubitsch

Mason Kamana Allred

LONDON AND NEW YORK

First published 2017 by Routledge

2 Park Square, Milton Park, Abingdon, Oxfordshire OX14 4RN
52 Vanderbilt Avenue, New York, NY 10017

Routledge is an imprint of the Taylor & Francis Group, an informa business

First issued in paperback 2019

Library of Congress Cataloging in Publication Data

CIP data has been applied for.

ISBN: 978-0-415-34918-5 (hbk)
ISBN: 978-0-367-88705-6 (pbk)

Typeset in Times New Roman
by diacriTech, Chennai

Contents

Acknowledgments

This book recognizes the fruitful interplay between different media, people, traditions, and history. In the same vein, I want to especially acknowledge the fruitful and enlightening history of conversations, support, and advice that contributed to its production. I am gratefully indebted to the inspiring community of minds at the University of California, Berkeley. Discussions with Anton Kaes, Chenxi Tang, Kristin Whissel, Linda Williams, Deniz Göktürk, Niklaus Largier, Karen Feldman, and Elaine Tennant were absolutely formative. Paul Dobryden, Nicholas Baer, Ben Bigelow, and Tyler Gardner were also important and encouraging interlocutors. Although all errors and flaws are solely my responsibility, the DNA of Berkeley and these minds shaped the work in a fundamental way.

The book also benefited from generous funding from UC-Berkeley as well as a Fulbright grant for a year stay in Germany. Much of the book began to take shape during that year in Berlin. Thanks to Gertrud Koch for hosting me at the Freie Universität and providing insights and challenges to my writing and thought. Sections of Chapter 1 were presented at the International Bremen Film Conference and appeared in German as part of *Film und Geschichte*, Winfried Pauleit, ed. (Bertz + Fischer, 2015). They are reprinted here with permission from the publisher.

I am grateful to the staff at Deutsche Kinemathek and the Bundesarchiv for their help and for granting me access to rare archival films and sources. Special thanks to Julia Riedel and Elisa Carl for help with the still images included herein.

Thanks to Felisa Salvago-Keyes and Christina Kowalski at Routledge for making the book's final stages such a joy. Their professionalism and support were stellar throughout the process.

I must thank Miya, Emi, and Ruka for joining in the journey to Berlin for a year, learning the language, and watching a lot of old silent German movies in their wise young age. Most of all thanks to Erika whose kind and perceptive ear I have been taxing with ideas—like the content of this book and beyond—for over a decade.

Introduction: Cinematic Historicity

"The principle of Goethe philology is that of *historicist* thinking, which emerged at about the same time as modern photographic technology."
—Siegfried Kracauer, 1927.[1]

The past has become cinematic. In its retrieval and (re)construction, the past has become intertwined with the images and structure of cinema. Not only have mass media, like film and television, shaped the content of memories and histories, but also their very form. Aristotle's definition of "fleeting" time as "a quantified and infinite *continuum* of precise fleeting instants"[2] was updated with new temporal structures of thought. Time, privately experienced, felt more fluid and reversible in the wake of cinema.[3] Once recorded and played back, time itself seemed to change and this effected way the past was conceived and represented across varying layers of historical culture. The Hungarian film theorist Béla Balázs sensed the shift when he "compared his remembrances of the past to film: individually motionless images yet, in their totality, moving pictures."[4] History became filtered through cinema.

As history is the deliberate reconstruction of the ever-mediated past, the craft of historiography also bares this transformative brushing with film. The world "stage of human history," became a screen of vivid, fragmented, and flickering images.[5] Stuck in the mindset of nations, historians have recently argued that our sense of the past changed after 1989, "after the collapse of the soviet bloc and the sudden end of the cold war."[6] But cinema had already exploded notions of borders, space, and time in a deeper sense and this book is about that change.

Much of this shift was due to cinema's ability to interact with the human body in ways print media could not. For many, the cultural sense of temporality and the access to the past gradually became imbued with a technological skeleton like the robot Maria in Fritz Lang's iconic silent film, *Metropolis* (1927). This technological apparatus that could present human surface (actors playing historical events) made recordings live again and again. But it could also represent historical imagination for mass embodied audiences. The human conception of temporality became mechanized and reproducible. The effect was that cinema provided a training ground for corporeal reaction and ritual in relation to a consumable historical image. This new training in temporality was part and parcel with the construction of a uniquely modern sense of historicity. What history was, felt like, meant, and did was affected by the medium of film and the practice of film viewing.

It would be difficult to overstate the significance of photographic media in the twentieth century, which was "unquestionably the century of cinema."[7] My focus here on film of the 1920s shaping historicity, experience, and the practice of historiography is a piece in a much larger puzzle. How the visual medium came to shape thought and experience in the twentieth century has only begun to be unfolded. The work of Doane,[8] Rosen,[9] Kittler,[10] Deleuze,[11] and Shaviro,[12] (to name a handful) all treat this development from diverse vantage points. As their work implies, the significance of analyzing the last century of film for the construction of popular and academic relations to the past lies in the power of cinema to affect other practices and media and that its influence stretches into our present.

The resonance of the early twentieth century in media history sounds in the realization that most "new media," as Rodowick has shown, still function with cinema as their guiding metaphor.[13] The Internet, personal computer, digital media, and global data have not eclipsed cinema's draw. As Manovich has recognized, "A hundred years after cinema's birth, cinematic ways of seeing the world, of structuring time, of narrating a story, of linking one experience to the next, have become the basic means by which computer users access and interact with all cultural data."[14] In fascinating ways, our present century, even in the digital age, remains rooted in the core practices born in the earlier years of film history.

Even in the first half of the twentieth century, the effects of the cinematic medium spanned the globe. Yet, methodologically zeroing-in on Weimar cinema and history reveals how local institutions and technologies reached diverse bodies of audiences and connected them internationally, forming a top-down history in the most inclusive form up till that point. Although local emphasis was possible and the body was seemingly relegated to the passive posture of sitting and gawking, these were both transformed in significant ways for the development of a filmic relationship to the past—to the experience of temporality itself. The ability of the cinematic medium to get viewing bodies involved and feeling was amplified by its penchant for making time plastic and malleable.

While this book focuses on Ernst Lubitsch's history films and the years 1919–1924—a relatively early moment in the history of film—this too is diachronically bound within a larger history of what might be called the "cinematic regime of historicity," which still deeply informs current relationships to the past. The intellectual historian and professor of historiography, Hartog, conceptualized the term "regime of historicity" to capture "the way in which a society considers its past and deals with it" or more broadly "the method of self-awareness in a human community." Much like the concept of "historical consciousness," used to study how people relate to and understand the past, a regime entails a horizon of possibilities of how societies experience and conceptualize historicity. Finally, in an effort to evoke the philosophical roots of the term, Hartog writes, "if ... historicity ... designates the 'condition of being, historically,' or yet 'humankind present to itself as history,' we will pay particular attention to the diversity of regimes of historicity."[15] The cinematic regime of historicity outlined in this book correlates with the emphasis on bodily experience of history. This semantic supplement to historiography and historical consciousness probes the relationship of technology and human experience in relation to time and history.

Historical moving pictures had much to do with understanding history through duration, by the *movement* of time, as well as the *motion* of the pictures themselves. These two components of historical film are also deeply imbricated. For this reason, it is important to realize that "We (adults) conceptualize time via deep, systematic, spatial-movement metaphors in which the passage of time is understood as relative to motion in space."[16] The embodied experience of movement and time came to inform the popular experience of history. Our bodies, the ground for comprehending duration and temporal difference, also became the ground for marking and representing "historical" time on screen. And this sense of time became an internationally shared conception through films like those of Lubitsch that traveled internationally.

The rise of cinema also affected important shifts in the relationship to space. Bygone and foreign spaces were represented on screen and made accessible, or at least viewable: history as ocular consumption. In many cases, the local became international and even global, while the body was called upon as the means and matter of insuring the possibility of experience. Another spatial outcome of the proliferation of filmed histories was a novel de/recontextualization. What did it mean to have Versailles reconstructed in Berlin or Ancient Egypt in the California desert? Since these ruptures of space were always meant for visual consumption, world history on film was always already for *everyone, everywhere*.

This shift in popular history coincided with "the organization of human sense perception and its transformation in industrial-capitalist modernity."[17] This book then offers an approach to analyzing the intersection of historicity and embodied reception by focusing on silent cinema in postwar

Germany. It helps to connect both the historical culture of popular film and the academy to the corporeal senses and sensations, which undergird the very construction *and* reception of history. The body was always the ground for envisioning history, but film made this carnal core come out of the closet. The millions of bodies craving sensational sights made up the international viewing public targeted by film industries like the mushrooming one in Germany.

Before all the technological accouterments of classical Hollywood epics, history on film was already a monumental undertaking in Germany. The years following the Great War signaled Germany's entry into the lucrative international market of historical filmmaking. Film—understood during the war as a means of influencing national sentiment at home—became a means of influencing relations and reputations abroad. While other scholars have treated, "[t]he flood of historical films that swamped the German cinema from 1919 to 1923–24," most have seen them, precisely as Eisner did, as "an expression of the escapism of a poverty-stricken, disappointed nation which, moreover, had always been fond of the glitter of parades."[18] They've neglected the films' historiographical force.

No scholarship to date has pursued the films' interaction with historicity or historiography, or how this interaction was inflected by bodily experience. Although he treats the history films of Ernst Lubitsch, Silberman focuses on the economic undertones tied to gender by recognizing the protagonist of *Passion* (1920) as a female commodity being exchanged between men. Yet, for Silberman, "Lubitsch is uninterested in events and historiography."[19] It follows that the film must be doing something else. McCormick sees an outsider's story of social mobility in historical costumes.[20] Elsaesser has located the political shift in German history toward transparency and democracy by approaching the film *Passion* with a Foucauldian lens. But Elsaesser adamantly directs the interpretation toward his concept of a "historical imaginary," away from historical imagination, which is connected to nineteenth century historiography.[21] The core treatment still remains Hake's monograph, *Passions and Deceptions*, from 1992. Hake provided important historicization and the most comprehensive overview of Lubitsch's late Berlin body of work. She perceptively portrayed Lubitsch's history films with the analogy of a palimpsest.[22] Hake reveals the films' ability to remain open to varied political readings, while engaging domestic issues. However, none of these treatments allow the history films to be films about history or symptomatic of shifts in historical experience.

Although each scholar has brought important insights into what the films might mean, a common thread through their treatments is a reluctance to consider the history films as historiographical—as writing history in any sense. Only allowing the films to mean anything but the history they portray, previous scholarship was often enveloped in early Memory Studies, and a focus on meaning making for the present moment. While the theoretical approach of collective memory helps to expose the shared character of pasts made present, it can also obscure the historiographical force of the films. The ability of the films to get into the viewer's bones and create experiential ties to the past carries connotations of memory studies, but a media studies focus on the role of film in shaping historicity carries the project beyond the memory paradigm.

The intervention in the following chapters helps to illuminate cinema's central position in the shift in historical understanding and experience. Initiating a trend in historical film viewing, the Lubitsch films treated here equally instigated significant cultural and political debates. The sheer volume of history films must have felt something like the current popular interest in superhero movies. The fascination stretched across continents. In fact, there were so many productions with historical subject matter on both sides of the Atlantic that Buster Keaton released his first feature-length comedy as a parallel structure of a man attempting to court women across three different historical periods. Titled, *Three Ages* and released in 1923, the film participated in, while parodying, the flare for historical scenes and detail, as the contemporary press described.

In 1923, *The New York Times* reported: "producers are directing their energies with amazing spontaneity" toward creating films with historical settings. There might be "one or a hundred reasons for this overwhelming wave of historical photoplays. Whenever and wherever the original germ of the idea may have been cast, it is evident that it proved highly contagious."[23] The possibilities of such a historical fervor went beyond mere profit. The writer stated with all the history films "the American public will be treated to a dramatic digest of the world's history and the half-forgotten memories of school books will be reawakened. It is safe to say that the second reading will be more pleasant than the first." In the spirit of D. W. Griffith, national film industries could foster historical learning, while filling their pockets and displaying their prosperity on screen.

Germany also desired an image of prosperity and cultural sophistication abroad. To this end, the new Weimar republic took measures to produce monumental films for export. Since the defeated German nation utilized the years immediately following the Great War to produce a "flood of historical films," to successfully catapult itself into the international film market, the moment provides a fruitful case study. It also bears potential for wider application. At the admitted neglect of many other films, I chose then to trace the impact and developments of cinematic historicity by primarily using the history films of Ernst Lubitsch as emblematic and expressive of this shift. As events and texts, *Madame Dubarry* (1919), *Anne Boleyn* (1920), and *Das Weib des Pharao* (1922) provide sturdy springboards for such analysis and historicization, especially because of their international reach and Lubitsch's unique play with visibility. In some ways, this simplifies and condenses a larger and longer process, but it serves to bring the discourses and phenomena into relief.

The chapters that follow do not chart a strict chronology or even linearity. Taking the years of 1919–1924 as a snapshot—a supremely telling moment—in the development of a cinematic relation to the past, the chapters jump between films and offer varied approaches to the same question: how did cinema shape the sense and embodied experience of history?

Chapters 1 and 2 revolve around moving history. In order to analyze the innovations of history films, both chapters also use the concept of a "frame," meaning in a concrete sense the frame of the shot and, figuratively, the audience's horizon of experience and thought, or frame of reference. By pushing these frames, Chapter 1 argues, history on film was meant to "move" people—to be viscerally and emotionally engaging. The initial chapter sets up the book's overarching argument that cinema made history into an experience for human bodies. This is accomplished by exploring the concept of *moving* experience in a qualified and limited way, since as Gadamer has observed, "However paradoxical it may seem, the concept of historical experience seems to me one of the most obscure we have."[24] By considering the frame of historical representation, Chapter 1 explores the bodily experience engendered by filmic history. Where a frame in history denotes the temporal space between the reader's present and the represented past, it also serves to highlight the (critical) distance between audience and history. Although this is a common objective approach in historicism, the films treated here do not employ such a strategy. Chapter 1 shows, rather, how historical film sought to return the human body to the historical process by representing it, fragmenting it, and, most importantly, appealing to it.

The ability of historical film to appeal to and specifically address an embodied audience requires some theoretical support. Chapter 1 then foreshadows developments in the preceding chapters by employing Frank Ankersmit's and Vivian Sobchack's notions of experience in relation to history, in order to argue for the value of the embodied experience of history on film. These conclusions build on conceptions of memory and history as bodily experience, an experience that is caught up in our flesh—even inscribed onto the human body. Audiences carry these histories around with them. The experience and images permeate thought about the past and even influence actions in the present, as the subsequent chapters will reveal.[25]

Chapter 2 recycles the concepts introduced in the opening chapter and is built around the idea that history on film "moved" to international contexts of reception. As an experience ultimately for bodies (regardless of nationality), history went international and, in so doing, posed important economic, political, and historiographical questions for the postwar German nation. This chapter treats the complexities of intertwining international audiences. It reveals how history films became entangled in existing national discourses, while emphatically addressing international bodies.

As a moving experience, the history shown on film posed important challenges for pedagogical and historiographical practice. Chapters 3 and 4 trace the institutional and intellectual responses to the medium and its effects. The reactions to historical film in the realm of education and the profession of history attest to the pervasive influence of cinematic experience on historical thinking. As a threat to deep, critical, distanced histories, film offered instead, surface, proximity, and experience. If historical thinking is an "unnatural act" that requires this critical distance, then film was threatening. Film instigated more than just ostensibly inaccurate content; it was equally subversive in its ability to teach perceiving bodies how to unlearn the unnatural act of historical thinking as *solely* historicism. Bodies viewing history films needed to be disciplined and educators and historians realized the potential pitfall of privileging bodily experience over cerebral engagement, even as it invaded their own relationship to the past.

Tracing embodiment and historicity as byproducts of a cinematic regime opens the door for alternative senses of the past: cinephilia, panoramic vision, technologically represented temporality, experience, and empathy through perception, for example. Emotionalizing and replaying stories of the past seem to betray or soften the critical rigor of historiography. Yet, it equally renders a realistic past, as it is lived and comprehensible—even usable—in the present. Lubitsch's oeuvre is especially well suited for this type of historical experience because of his style of self-reflexivity and play, alongside serious attention to detail, subtlety, and overt artificiality. While perhaps not deliberately in the historiographical mode, Lubitsch was clearly self-conscious in his approach to representation and the power of objects and surface. This combination produced films that could shake up historical sense(s).

As a reaction to such cinematic conventions, the pedagogical and historicist engagements and, at times, dismissal of history on film help to highlight the productive paradox at work in the early twentieth century. Many scholars have continued the tradition today, even maintaining some of the language, of debating the in/ability of film to do history. The tension would not exist if it were not for the rise of nineteenth-century historicism and its powerful grip on the western world. Because film could function as both fulfillment and reaction to historicism, it was particularly potent. In this way, rather than argue if film is "history" or not, it is helpful to pull back from the canvas and take in a broader view of how historical film actually works and why such a tension can never be "worked out." Such an approach reveals how history on film functions, in many ways, as historicism's unconscious, revealing its issues, potential, and dreams.

Notes

1 Siegfried Kracauer, *The Mass Ornament: Weimar Essays* (Cambridge, MA: Harvard University Press, 1995), 49.
2 Giorgio Agamben, *Infancy and History: The Destruction of Experience*, trans. Liz Heron (London: Verso, 1993), 93. See also Chris Lorenz, "Unstuck in Time" in *Performing the Past: Memory, History, and Identity in Modern Europe*, eds. Karin Tilmans, Frank van Vree, and J. M. Winter (Amsterdam: Amsterdam University Press, 2010), 76.
3 Stephen Kern, *The Culture of Time and Space, 1880–1918: With a New Preface*, 2nd ed. (Cambridge, MA: Harvard University Press, 2003), 34.
4 Joseph Zsuffa, *Béla Balázs: The Man and the Artist* (Oakland, CA: University of California Press, 1987), 57.
5 See Eduardo Cadava, *Words of Light: Theses on the Photography of History* (Princeton, NJ: Princeton University Press, 1997), xviii–xix.
6 Lorenz, "Unstuck in Time," 67.
7 David Norman Rodowick, *The Virtual Life of Film* (Cambridge, MA: Harvard University Press, 2009), 2.
8 Mary Ann Doane, *The Emergence of Cinematic Time: Modernity, Contingency, the Archive* (Cambridge, MA: Harvard University Press, 2002).
9 Philip Rosen, *Change Mummified: Cinema, Historicity, Theory* (Minneapolis, MN: University of Minnesota Press, 2001), xi-xxv.
10 Friedrich A. Kittler, *Gramophone, Film, Typewriter* (Redwood City, CA: Stanford University Press, 1999).
11 Gilles Deleuze, *Cinema: The Time-Image* (Minneapolis, MN: University of Minnesota Press, 1989).
12 Steven Shaviro, *Post Cinematic Affect* (New York, NY: Zero Books, 2010).
13 Rodowick, *The Virtual Life of Film*, viii.
14 Lev Manovich, *The Language of New Media* (Cambridge, MA: MIT Press, 2001), 78–79.
15 François Hartog, "Time and Heritage," *Museum International* 57, no. 3 (2005): 8.
16 Mark Johnson, *The Meaning of the Body: Aesthetics of Human Understanding* (Chicago: University of Chicago Press, 2007), 28.
17 Miriam Bratu Hansen, *Cinema and Experience: Siegfried Kracauer, Walter Benjamin, and Theodor W. Adorno* (Oakland, CA: University of California Press, 2011), 4.
18 Lotte H. Eisner, *The Haunted Screen: Expressionism in the German Cinema and the Influence of Max Reinhardt* (Oakland, CA: University of California Press, 1969), 75.
19 Marc Silberman, "Revolution, Power, and Desire in Ernst Lubitsch's *Madame Dubarry*," in *Expressionist Film: New Perspectives*, ed. Dietrich Scheunemann (Rochester, NY: Camden House, 2003), 74–75.
20 Richard McCormick, "Sex, History, and Upward Mobility: Ernst Lubitsch's Madame Dubarry/Passion, 1919," *German Studies Review* 33, no. 3 (October 2010): 603–17.

21 Thoma Elsaesser, *Weimar Cinema and After: Germany's Historical Imaginary* (London: Routledge, 2000), 195–222.

22 Sabine Hake, *Passions and Deceptions: The Early Films of Ernst Lubitsch* (Princeton, NJ: Princeton University Press, 1992), 117. Kristin Thompson has also provided in-depth analysis of Lubitsch's films from this period, but it is much more focused on technical developments. See *Herr Lubitsch goes to Hollywood* (Amsterdam: Amsterdam University Press, 2005).

23 *New York Times*, "Producers Busy With History's High Spots: Ripping Up Histories" July 25, 1923, WF4.

24 Hans-Georg Gadamer, *Truth and Method* (London: Continuum, 2004), 341.

25 Alison Landsberg, *Prosthetic Memory: The Transformation of American Remembrance in the Age of Mass Culture* (New York, NY: Columbia University Press, 2004).

1 Screening Pasts through Carnal Presence

"We think that we don't believe in a bunch of things with our intellect, but our body still believes in them, and it is always more powerful."
—Egon Friedell, 1921[1]

When *The Execution of Mary, Queen of Scots* was staged as a fully "fleshed-out" beheading on film in 1895, the distinct elements of visualizing history and appealing to the body were combined.[2] The early historical film, with severe time constraints and budgetary limitations, realized the most bang for the buck was to stage a scene of gruesome history. The trick film's eighteen seconds include costumed historical figures at the site of a beheading and conclude with a masked executioner lifting the queen's severed head triumphantly for the full view of the camera. The exploitative potential of historical film was already evident at its inception.[3] Always interested in addressing bodily concerns, it is no surprise that nearly twenty-five years later, the German director Ernst Lubitsch ended his film of the French Revolution with Madame Dubarry's grisly execution at the Guillotine. Lubitsch's film presented bodily fragmentation as historical display for audiences already over two decades into their habituation to cinematic experience.

In the final scene of *Madame Dubarry* (1919), a matte shot parts like a curtain and the camera positions the audience in an iconic relationship with the yelling masses on screen (see Figures 1.1 and 1.2). The platform of the guillotine is, like the screen in the cinema, slightly elevated and the clear center of attention. In the American edit, Dubarry pleads, "One moment more. Life is so sweet," reminding the audience of just what is at stake when temporality and fatality collide. The film displays Dubarry being strapped to the death machine and then abruptly cuts to the candle representing her glowing life, as it is extinguished. In the original German version, no title cards invade the screen to prolong Dubarry's life. The film simply cuts to a close-up of the blade plummeting down the frame. The blade drops, closing the contraption's cavity for a head, recalling the fact that "the term

Figure 1.1 Eager for a spectacle, the masses congregate and yell around the guillotine platform. *Madame Dubarry*, 1919. Image courtesy of Stiftung
Deutsche Kinemathek, Berlin.

'guillotine' also refers to a kind of drop shutter found in nineteenth-century
cameras"[4] and that the technical term for the executioner even became "photographer."[5] Putting these elements into motion the film continues, cutting
from the blade to a long shot of the executioner, or photographer, retriev-
ing Dubarry's head from the platform. He then tosses the severed head to
the ecstatic crowd and a final close-up reveals the head, captured by living
hands and the magic of film. History is placed in the hands of the masses.

Such depictions of historical bodies, in grave and sensational settings,
constituted a qualitatively new mode of history that appealed to modern
embodied viewers. Whereas, traditional historicism should edit the human
body out of the historical process through "Selbstauslöschung" (or extin-
guishing of self for objectivity),[6] film functioned precisely by appealing to
the emotions, movements, and experiences of audience's bodies. History
on film engaged audiences in their material reality—in their "skin and
hair."[7] Allowing an embodied audience to view and experience historical
bodies fragmented on screen, whether through simulated dismemberment

Figure 1.2 Dubarry faces her executioner. *Madame Dubarry*, 1919. Image
    courtesy of Stiftung Deutsche Kinemathek, Berlin.

or editing techniques, updated the cultural sense of history. This was the
carnally charged history reaching audiences across the globe and eclipsing
novels, monographs, and magazines.

For more critical viewers, such portrayals of the past were difficult to accept
as history. In his 1947 assessment of Weimar German film, cultural critic
Kracauer described Lubitsch's history films, in particular, as "nihilistic." For
Kracauer, Lubitsch's "cynicism and melodramatic sentimentality … characterized history as meaningless."[8] The type of history produced by Lubitsch
could certainly be construed as irresponsible or even meaningless, yet it
is the very "spectatorial experience that resists co-optation by meaning"
that produced a radically modern type of history.[9] Recognizing the potential threat of what appears under the lens of historicism as "soft" history,[10]
it is nevertheless necessary to investigate the experience of such a meta-
phorically textured approach to the past, especially considering the films'
international reach and ubiquity. This chapter then uses the reception and
event of *Madame Dubarry* to traverse the modern, cinematically structured
historical experience that historicism methodologically neglects.

What follows is not an attack on historicism and its emphasis on narrative. To be sure, the presence of historicism or other strands of academic history is necessary. These serve as reflective structures in a discursive realm that can orient the present in empirical ways. They can also serve the important function of correcting dangerous inaccuracies of looser engagements with the past, which films generally pursue. In this way, academic historical discourse works to "correct, critique, or even include" film as it does with collective memory.[11] The subsequent chapters will further treat this constant appeal to historicism in order to understand cinematic history. However, as Paul Riceour insightfully concedes, although "history can expand, complete, correct, even refute the testimony of memory" (and I would include here films) "regarding the past; it cannot abolish it."[12]

The precise way in which historical films came to appeal to the human body for experiencing what is "historical" helps to highlight the significant role of cinema in the construction of a cinematic regime of historicity. The technological and historically specific mode of address suffusing this experience produced "new history," by updating history's reception through the cinematic medium. To this end, it is helpful to revisit Kracauer's trepidation toward photography and history (before his damning analysis of Lubitsch's films after World War II). Doing so elucidates how Lubitsch's history of Madame Dubarry, as a typification of the genre of history film at the time, may have been cynical and even sentimental, but made history sensual, specifically for modern embodied viewers.

Thawing Historicism

Kracauer's valid concern with the photographic medium was that it only offers surface and thereby buries history "under a layer of snow." Because of the ontological realism of the camera, this blizzard effect would be the inevitable result if only Lubitsch-type history films were linking present to past. For Kracauer, these couldn't do real history since the historian's task, as he later articulated it, lies in "penetrating [the past's] outward appearance, so that he may learn to understand that world from within."[13] By only providing the outward appearance, the destructive and eclipsing forces of photographic media were "sweeping away the dams of memory."[14] Even though these media showed more, society came to know less.

Whereas Kracauer's concern with Lubitsch's films in 1947 was narrative implication, his interwar reflection was based on the medium itself. This is an important distinction in the effort to describe historical experience rather than the "meaning" of historical accounts *per se*. Certainly, for a German émigré after World War II, the meaning and narrative of history films could not be ignored. His focus on finding the rise of Hitler in feature films clouded his earlier radical reflections. But, as Kracauer had realized in the 1920s, the problem preceding narrative was that although the blizzard effect created an opportunity for new encounters with nature the unacceptable trade-off was surface, a mere "spatial continuum."

On the other hand, the historicist tradition, stemming from the Enlightenment, precipitated its own blizzard effect. As Dutch Novelist Nicolaas Beets put it, "the temperature decreased from that of human blood to that of frost. It literally snowed big ideas. It was a fresh but, in the end, uncomfortable cold."[15] This chilling historicism banished the experience of the past in favor of objectivity and distinction. The necessary critical distance was achieved through the emphatic construction of a "frame" between past and present. Like the frame of an artwork, this temporal frame kept the past at bay, as an object of study. By creating concepts like nation, state, era, and century and by eschewing notation in favor of pure predictive writing, historiography after the "Enlightenment" (an important example of one such creation) emphasized the difference and distance between past and present.[16] Even if the past only led to the present, they were divided by the past's very narration.

Recent scholarship on "collective memory," especially since Pierre Nora's and Yosef Yerushalmi's groundbreaking studies, gives credence to this cold characterization of historicism that supplanted more intimate and experiential ties to the past.[17] In similar terms, Beet's conception of the Enlightenment and historicism was a cold, scientific, negative disenchantment of the world, whereas Kracauer's photographic snow represented the loss of depth and distinguishing traits concealed under a "jumble that consists partially of garbage."[18] Both Beets' and Kracauer's forecasts, while revealing the limits of each mode of representing the past, were metaphorical polarities devoid of carnality, experience, and sensation. Where photography required no human intervention, historicism privileged logical thought over affect. Both poles extracted the warmth of sensing bodies in the historical process.

Set against the freezing pole of historicism, Dutch historical theorist Ankersmit has recently explored what he terms "subjective" and "sublime" historical experience. He explicitly stated his aim as replacing "the intellectual bureaucracy of 'theory'" with a "romantic" notion of experience. By turning away from a focus on narrative and textuality, Ankersmit celebrates the way the historian, as an "oracle" of sorts, works through personal historical experience to produce historiography. Maintaining the elitist focus on historians as the practitioners of history, Ankersmit describes this process as occurring in the historian's mind, where "the drama of world history is enacted."[19] Thus, the historical experience, germinating in the imagination, precedes narrative and linguistic articulation. It is also clear that history is always something that is subjectively "seen," whether it becomes translated and disciplined into historiography or not.

Ankersmit's work represents a major shift from his earlier narratological studies and helps to validate and envision subjective prelinguistic experience as a mode of history. Although he clearly does not have film in mind, with silent historical film, an increasingly international audience was experiencing historical drama enacted before their eyes (and bodies). As the growing primary means for the public to engage the past in sensory ways, cinematic historicity became a regime in itself—one that informs structures of thought and feelings about the past—and requires its own historicization. And in this sense, Ankersmit probably *does* have film in mind, whether he realizes it or not, as most have become embedded in an overwhelmingly cinematic relationship to the past.[20]

In order to more closely examine this process of silent film inflecting historical experience, Sobchack's phenomenological film theory proves illuminating. Sobchack primarily invokes Merleau-Ponty in her analysis, since he was a key figure in shifting the focus of experience from consciousness to the body. Sobchack's emphasis on the body as the site of cross-modal sensory reception helps to reconcile Kracauer's mere surface (of the photographic medium) with his recognition in 1960 that "film images affect primarily the spectator's senses ... engaging him physiologically before ... intellectually"[21] and his conviction that "[t]he film experience involves 'not so much [the spectator's] power of reasoning as his visceral faculties,' his 'sense organs.'"[22] In this theoretical light, Lubitsch's *Madame Dubarry* stoked the human body and blood to make historical sense through sensory experience. Embodied audiences were furnished with opportunities to have "subjective historical experiences" in Ankersmit's terminology, which offered something of the feel and look of the past, including its spatial configuration (in rooms, choreography, and architecture) and texture. The shift from textual to textural not only describes this theoretical framework but the film's rendering of the past.[23]

Historical Sense

Despite its focus on texture, texts are certainly not absent in *Madame Dubarry*. Thirteen times the screen is filled with a historical document, functioning as a title card. On a formal level, the living historical characters enter the screen from these texts only to subsume them with their hand, pocket, or even bosom. The technique is brought to a sensual climax during the initial encounter between King Louis XV and Dubarry. After gazing at Dubarry's cleavage, the king discovers a rolled-up document between her breasts. Once he has removed the document, we read the petition through the king's point of view, he then signs and returns it to the same "historic" breasts (see Figure 1.3). At this point, the document visually fades into the human figure. The conventional object of historicism (text) is subsumed, with sexual overtones, into the living historical figure (sensual image). This also exemplifies the translation of historiography into the increasingly universal language of film and into a new regime of historicity, one that is wrapped up with the photographic medium and understands history in its visibility and texture.

The cinematic experience shifts our focus from that document's narrative implications to the viewer's ability to, like the figure of Dubarry on screen, feel, sense, and perceive something before and after the text. While there is, obviously, no tangible document slid from and returned to viewers' chests, the audience is invited to feel the text as texture in a diffused sense, "on the rebound."[24] The feeling on screen, literally depicted in its visibility, returns the audience to feel their own physical presence and embodiment, to feel themselves feeling. This means the experience of historical texts translated into film touches or moves the body in ways that elicit a response, as embodied and enacted by Dubarry on screen. Before we witness her lose her head, we watch Dubarry giggle and jiggle as the document is returned to her chest. Texture and bodies, both sexualized and severed, serve to create moving history.

Figure 1.3 Bodies and texts interact as King Louis XV retrieves a document from Dubarry's chest. *Madame Dubarry*, 1919. Image courtesy of Stiftung Deutsche Kinemathek, Berlin.

The experience of the scene also encapsulates a fleshy wearing of history, as it becomes inscribed onto the body through sensual mediation. This tactile experience of cinema, in general, surfaced in author and political activist, Mierendorff's 1920 description of attending a movie when he wrote, "The film unwinds; now the man up there on the screen pounces on the woman. Down below, every woman feels pounced on, every man pounces."[25] Mierendorff's formulation is an important attempt to put into language what was occurring before language—to describe the prelinguistic sense of film spectatorship. Where one might use "mirror neurons"[26] to explain such phenomena today, the visceral reaction to images on screen was already understood in Weimar culture as crossmodal stimulation.

In 1914, Hellwig, a German lawyer with a scholarly interest in film, summarized recent research in Italy to support his observations about olfactory, aural, and haptic responses to silent films. The "hallucinations" and "illusions" experienced by audiences evidenced the powerful grip film images had on the body. It had been "found that under the influence of cinematic projections, spectators interpreted other sense impressions in such a way as to associate them with the events shown in the moving image." Several cases had been confirmed, "in which, in the absence of any sense impression beyond that of the projection itself, spectators imagined impressions to go with the events on the screen." Even the good doctors themselves were surprisingly susceptible to such crossmodal perception of films. During one such research screening, the film displayed a stable full of hay. At the appearance of the hay, "Professor Kiesow remarked to Dr. Ponzo that it was as if he could smell the hay—and this just as Ponzo was turning toward Professor Kiesow to make the same remark."[27] This fascinating effect of synesthesia was, for Hellwig, something "all of us have probably experienced while attending cinematic projections." Hellwig could generalize the ubiquity of the illusions since audiences are "particularly susceptible to them in those moments when we abandon ourselves completely to the representation" on screen. For attentive observers, it was clear that rather than completely negating bodily perception, films actually engaged the skin, stomach, ears, and pulse *through* the eyes.

The attempt to put the experience of film into words and analysis highlights the nearly ineffable magic of film viewing and this had significant ramifications for history. History films, in particular, could deploy varied generic conventions to elicit reactions in the audience, like Mierendorff and the researchers had. The reproducible medium could replicate responses and effects. Since history films often flirted with the elements of horror, melodrama, and eroticism they borrowed from and helped establish the "body genres," or those most explicitly (excessively) "jerking" bodily reactions from the audience.[28] These methods of enlisting the body also informed the sense of the past. The sense of history was tied up with the audience's bodily experience of the representation, before it spilled over into reflection. This new cinematic flavor of history was magnified by Lubitsch's continual foregrounding of surface over depth. As Silberman has described it, "[t]ypically in *Passion* historical event is displaced to the margins and historical ornament (dress, gesture, and décor) dominate the mise-en-scenè ... aesthetics and artifice dominate the film's visual style."[29] What was "historical" was increasingly married to experience through vision, rather than narrative reflection. History was thus, truly "decaying into images, not stories."[30]

The images in *Madame Dubarry* engendered experience in a "prere-flective, popular, and 'undisciplined' manner," by sensually recounting the dramatized history of the French Revolution.[31] Although the focus should remain on image and experience, a brief synopsis of the film is in order. Largely lifted from a Viennese operetta, the plot of *Madame Dubarry* traces the social rise of the milliner's apprentice, Jeanne Vaubernier, as she enters the realm of politics and sexual intrigue, essentially romancing her way to the court as King Louis XV's mistress. In order for the King to receive Jeanne at court, she becomes Madame Dubarry through a staged marriage to the, otherwise useless, Count Dubarry. Jeanne's newfound political clout allows her to protect her earlier lover, the commoner and revolutionary Armand De Foix. After the king dies of smallpox, his scheming minister, Choiseul, has Madame Dubarry officially banished from Paris. Left to fend for herself, Madame Dubarry is captured by the growing mob and sentenced to death by her beloved Armand, who sits in judgment at her trial. Although Armand disguises himself and attempts to rescue Dubarry from her cell, he is discovered and shot. In the final scene, Dubarry is led to her death at the guillotine.

Narratively, this was fitting subject matter, since it was precisely, as Lukacs observed, "the French Revolution, the revolutionary wars and the rise and fall of Napoleon, which for the first time made history a mass expe-rience."[32] There exists, of course, a visual connection between spectacle in the eighteenth century and cinema spectatorship in the twentieth. As both were able to offer "history in the making" for a mass audience, their conflu-ence further underscored the significance of revolution as spectacle. In early Weimar, the French Revolution was already loaded with varied political, historical, and cultural meanings, and therefore ripe for present use. Not only were the streets of Berlin often full of revolting masses, but the recent stilted inauguration of the Weimar republic resonated in the film's subject matter and choreography of crowds. And the film's reception at home and abroad indicated the development of another revolution—a media revolu-tion in the popular experience of history.[33]

Inspired by his viewing of *Dubarry*, the Austrian journalist and theater critic, Friedell linked the film's representation of a historical revolution to mankind's revolutionary development of new historical understanding. Finally, enabled to comprehend the importance of just such a revolution humans could translate understanding into action. This kind of carnal historical knowing was not possible as an actor, a contemporary figure, within the revolution itself. Through the temporal and visual distance afforded history on film, "movements" could gain certain "clarity" and they seem almost "quicker, than they were in reality, which only simplifies their comprehension."[34] The effect of cinema in presenting a history that was at once distant and objectively visible, and yet so close it entered the nervous system of the spectator through perception, was truly groundbreaking. But the effect required proper cinematic execution.

Friedell credited Lubitsch with successfully making the French Revolution "Filmreif," or truly cinematic material, by aestheticizing such a destructive rupture in history. Condensing and concentrating the revolution in the filmic form, as Lubitsch had achieved, the lively corporeal display could forge a revolutionary understanding of the intellect (upon reflection) as well as the nerves and body. Here, Friedell not only anticipated Benjamin's concept of collective instruction through shocks, but also Kracauer's understanding of the "role of cinematic movement, speed, and multiple and rapidly changing viewpoints in updating human consciousness and the sensorium to the level of technology; as well as film's affinity with the scale and movement of huge crowds and the experience of chance (as opposed to fate and providence), which gains significance with the 'entry of the masses into history.'"[35]

Friedell sensed the significance of the international blockbuster that visualized Dubarry's sexy life and grisly death. With filmed histories like *Dubarry*, cinemas became training grounds, engraining a corporeal sense of the past, which should then "catch up" with the mind. While the reflective spectator could question, wonder, and learn from such experiences, the body itself was learning to cope with the new history.

This new sense of history was unlike written histories. It is true that even *Dubarry* was no exception to Rosen's point, that research has ever been an integral aspect of historical filmmaking.[36] The film was seen to bear exquisite period detail and Pola Negri "[threw] herself into research ... trying to extract the essence of the character [of madame Dubarry]," while Emil Jannings had "endless conversations"[37] with Lubitsch over the nature of Louis XV, yet the film sidestepped historicist methodological explication.[38] Instead, the film followed the generic tradition and focused on the entertaining and sensory experience of that imagined past's look and feel.[39] Therefore, rather than pursue film's ability to write history on film, it is productive to highlight the novelty of the sensory experience of the past—one that sought to foreground the body through modern technology.[40] That is to say, history films, like *Dubarry*, have always been manufactured not only for the present, but also for bodily *presence*. The resulting experience of this corporeal focus, implicated in but more significant than the reality effect, might be the pinnacle of how historical film functions in the construction of historicity.

There is, however, a long-standing concern with ideology and power as it relates to dramatized history on film. Certainly, the lack of revolutionary power in *Madame Dubarry's* narrative was the impetus for Kracuaer's dismissal. Yet, Kracauer's treatment emphasized national needs and judged Lubitsch's film as if the latter were "a historian of the 'historical imagination,'" coinciding with historicism.[41] The rigor of historicism and the construction of national identity may not be the most productive approaches in unpacking *Madame Dubarry's* cultural force. The turn to historical experience tempers the traditional focus on historical fidelity. Since the experience of history "escapes the intellectual matrix of historical truth and representation," the object of analysis is not film's (in)ability to write the past on historicism's terms.[42] It is rather, the far-reaching construction of a relationship to the past, structured by the medium of film and its powerful images.

This line of inquiry echoes Ankersmit's admission that "how we *feel* about the past is no less important than what we know about it—and probably even more so."[43] For this reason, it "makes no sense to analyze historical consciousness or awareness in terms of truth and falsity."[44] The circumvention of critical theory in order to recuperate notions of historical experience is thorny and fraught with a certain abandon; however, the attempt necessarily moves us beyond textuality and debates over accuracy to the question of how historicity is culturally constructed and what the bodily and experiential link to the past might offer. Since this experience came to, more than any other form, shape modern-day historical consciousness on a popular level, the historical specificity of *Madame Dubarry's* reception has contemporary significance. By investigating the popular level of consuming and constructing history and experience the "means by which publics develop their sense of the past, can be appreciated more fully."[45]

In the movie palaces at home and abroad, the history on film of the 1920s was working to create an embodied experience of the past. Without cinemascope, color, or synched sound *Madame Dubarry* made the past sensual. In order to get viewers "caught up in a comprehension of time … in which to sense [themselves] as temporal beings who transcend [their] present presence," *Dubarry* wrote history on the senses through the use of excess, repetition, and length. These served to literalize, multiply, and translate culturally determined notions of temporality and historicity into an embodied experience.

Wearing History

A primary means to create historical sense was achieved through the deployment of material, as well as temporal, excess. Excess, as a formally conditional term based on exceeding expectations of genre and cinematic precedence, could transmute cultural conceptions of history. Big stars, costumes, and sets should signal to viewing bodies the magnitude and dimensions of history. Without the elephants of *Cabiria* and *Intolerance*, Lubitsch turned to other means of signifying excess.[46] The casting of *Dubarry* with Emil Jannings and Pola Negri conferred a certain gravity upon the historical figures they embodied and the film brought them both international fame. In 1919, it was already recognized that films were strategically "wrapped around their stars like custom-made clothing."[47] And these attractive stars were just as impressively wrapped in costuming, which showcased historical attire in motion, as in a Berlin fashion show.[48] Lubitsch, as the son of a tailor and director of several "fashion farces," was as qualified as any to literally fill the screen with sumptuous textures of the past. The visual magnitude of historical dress, displayed like so many swatches in motion, signified an abundance that was tied to the importance of the staged temporality.

Costuming was itself a spectacle because, as Rosenstone has observed, "in film, period clothing does not hang limply on a dummy in a glass case, as it does in a museum; rather, it confines, emphasizes, and expresses the moving body."[49] Stars draped in period clothing piqued the historical experience of audiences. The images offered absorption in makeup and dress that were constructed for visual reception, whereby they are nearly felt as historical restraints on the viewing human body. The focus on material also bled into other Lubitsch creations like his mythical tale in Arabia, *Sumurun* of 1920. In this film, the Sheik's headmistress falls in love with a cloth merchant and textiles continually punctuate the scenery. In fact, the silky cloths even become metonymic vessels, within which Lubitsch transfers the sexual desire between Sumurun and the salesmen, by focusing on close-ups of the pair's hands as they caress the silky material between them. The textured surface of cloth also becomes sexually charged through potential opportunities for dressing and undressing. By framing cloth with desire and tactility, the films, then, bear clear continuities with Lubitsch's earlier fashion farces. These had helped democratize the elitist experience of the fashion show and "engaged the senses, molded the tastes, [and] influenced everyday practices … for mass viewers."[50]

The ornate style of dress in Lubitsch's *Dubarry* was also connected to the fashion industry. History films of the postwar era coincided with and shaped interest in period dress for upscale parties. Such costuming and play with appearance were part of larger divisions in class and gender and helped spark the evolution of the brassiere.[51] Innovative bras were also a material issue, since the diminishing use of corsets had freed up much-needed metal resources for the war. Yet, in 1921, French fashion designer Paul Poiret emphasized the need for adapted corsets because, "if women wear corsets they can wear the dresses of King Louis XV, and the eighteenth century styles. Minus corsets that will be impossible."[52] The cover of *Vogue* in 1921 also showcased the latest styles and the standout novelty of the issue was the extravagant period dress. "You will be able to make up your mind about 'period dresses,' too and decide whether they are suited for your type or not," stated the illustrated advertisement.[53] Although the emergence of flapper styles and art-deco inspired simplicity were beginning to dominate women's popular fashion, there existed a surprising myriad of "clever ideas, old and new" including "revivalisms and theatrical costume influences."[54] Designers continued to garner inspiration from period pieces by reintroducing "the bustle, cinched waistline, and the high collar, to name but a few," through the twenties and into the thirties.[55] Revival fashion could work with the movies to market styles that would extend the experience in the theater and couple the past with current conspicuous consumption.

In *Dubarry*, the interplay of historical bodies and clothing is emphasized through framing, wardrobe changes, and the frequent appearance/disappearance of bodies. This is intensified during one scene, as we watch King Louis passionately watching Jeanne dress behind a screen and become aware of our own bodies watching historical bodies (un)dress. It is also no coincidence that Jeanne masquerades in men's clothing to surreptitiously visit Armand or that Armand later disguises himself as a priest in an attempt to rescue Jeanne. All this play with textile emphasizes the historical body as much as meticulous costuming.

At one point, the camera angle rises in a seductive tilt shot revealing the thick embroidered train of Dubarry's dress. A pair of dark hands is shown in close-up flattening and caressing the silky material until the index of royal cloth leads the viewer to the head of Dubarry herself. Since, as architect Pallasmaa reminds us, "[t]ouch is the unconsciousness of vision, and this hidden tactile experience determines the sensuous quality of the perceived object," seeing the cloth handled on-screen structures a cinematic touching with the eyes.[56] Such cinematic framing of haptic history allows for the vicarious experience of period clothing and this requires that bodies are just as emphasized as what they wear.

By clothing bodies with history, the film doubles the cinematic apparatus itself, which covers the past (like snow) with a surface. The importance of bodies on screen also fueled the desire for history with flesh. Similar to the decapitation's ability to foreground the viewer's body through visceral reaction, the framing of history with sultry women and beefcake brawns shaped a type of "muscle memory" that made historical figures into the bodies audiences want to look at. Not only would viewing bodies become accustomed to the cinematic form of aesthetic history, but the actors' bodies presented on screen filled the audience's voluntary memory—"wearing" the historical period, title, and event. From Maciste to Siegfried and Tarzan, men's flesh was just as necessary as women's in getting bodies into the theater. The original posters for *Dubarry* depicted a grand physical struggle before a shirtless executioner. Even more emphasized than Dubarry, the masculine behemoth of flesh stands as a focal point in the scene in the film as well. He is the muscle capable of ending her life. Even with the modern technology of a guillotine, the organic body of the executioner had to be present as part of the spectacle. Dubarry's body drips down the posters like a Dali clock, hung on the branches of her tormentors. And artist Theo Matejko even rendered her top open, exposing her breasts for the Austrian version, while darkening the skin color of the executioner. The posters' magnification of the film's fleshy ending reminds us that it was never just beautiful dress that made history appealing and experiential. Neither was it because film images are pure surface. Both constructions of desire hinge on an understanding, and often a peepshow corroboration, that there exists something of substance under the surface display.

The effect of linking bodies with sensual dress also occurs at a ball inside the Paris Opera where elegant attire whirls in and out of the frame. The magnitude of such scenes is encapsulated in Lubitsch's formal play with convention. The ball begins with a montage-like series of frenetic and overflowing scenes of Paris' upper crust dancing and drinking, before the camera lingers on a pair of feet. The matted close-up of Dubarry's dangling feet reflects the gaze of the dancers and the audience. Like her eventual execution, this edit fragments Jeanne's body in order to securely couple it with visual consumption. Only after establishing the "to-be-looked-at" ness of Dubarry's legs does the film dissolve the matte to reveal a wide shot of the hall swarming with embodied costumes dancing in time. Capturing the costumes, as well as the dance hall, on film impresses the viewer as an historic obstacle in its own right.

Pushing the limits of the frame with bodies and textiles signaled the historicity and importance of the material. The "temporal *magnitude*" in *Dubarry* was "constituted not only by the 'big' presence of stars but also by literal *quantity*." Excess in *Dubarry* visually realized, for perceiving bodies, the "culturally sedimented" conception that "History is made literal and material through *scale*."[57] Beyond the meticulous attention to clothing, *Dubarry* made the French Revolution historical through its portrayal of sheer masses of people. The otherwise unemployed hordes of extras on screen in historical attire provided an interesting "material basis."[58] Lubitsch used this workforce to create the sense of quantity by strategically choreographing and framing his extras. Often flowing in and out of the shot, the mobs can almost seem infinite. The framing of unprecedented quantity and spectacle emphasized the magnitude of history for embodied urban viewers familiar with crowds. "No one before" had done it like Lubitsch.[59]

Striving to signal history, by "reaching [the] limits of excellence," historical film pushed for experience.[60] The sensory impact of this excess urged the audience's consciousness to reach beyond their own temporal frame and sense the (very real) existence and significance of other temporalities. This experience helped realize Dilthey's insight, in the nineteenth century, that the relationship to historical consciousness is one of "comparison of self with others" and the extrapolation of "an inside" to the initial surface "complex of external sensory signs."[61] As excess on the limits could push their mind into offscreen space, the figures on screen, as bodies like them, could also get viewers caught up in a deep sense of the reality of other times and peoples. Using the edges of the shot frame realized that, whereas "[f]ocused vision makes us mere outside observers; peripheral perception transforms retinal images into a spatial and bodily involvement and encourages participation."[62] This had consequences for international connections, which the next chapter will reveal, but also for individual perceptions of immersive experience.

Filling the frame with notation, or excessive details, unnecessary for traditional historiography, helped to ensure experience by downplaying the temporal frame or by thematizing it as a surmountable construction. The ability, however, to mobilize the limits of a visual shot as an experience that paralleled present moment of viewing with past (imagined) moments was contingent upon the existence of the frame in the first place. Like notational modes of history writing, experiential history films exploited and relied on the "frames" and constructions already promulgated by nineteenth-century-style historicism. In other words, the thrilling experience of notation, as excessive reality effects, worked only "in contrast with prediction and meaning."[63]

While *Dubarry* could "mean" many different things to different audiences, it often works to make history one of effects and artifacts for a perceiving body. The German reviewer for *Lichtbild Bühne* began his comments on *Dubarry* from the effect of the extreme detail, by stating the viewer is "first enraptured, by outward appearance alone, the period costuming, the authenticity of the milieu, constructed with incomparable accuracy."[64] In the many lists of effects and virtues, the linguistic organization of the experience also tended to take on the form of cataloguing, so integral to nineteenth-century historicism and literary realism.[65] The recognition of so much notation and detail on screen initiated the impulse to recount the many effects in succession. The American praise for the film's "historical real-ism," so derided by Kracauer as a naïve "craving for history debunked,"[66] also speaks to the reflective and linguistic means of explaining the effect and affect of magnitude on screen. The excess worked primarily in a prere-flective manner to make historicity felt, as spectacle in the form of modern shock. For modern subjects, in the present moment of viewing, magnitude, scale, and detail in excess felt "historical."

Enduring Duration

Focusing on the temporal excess in Lubitsch's history films brings their convoluted plots and dramatic volatility into relief. The countless ups and downs, usually including death and battle, were in some measure due to duration. The course of a history film itself often represented a historical life and usually ended in death. Dubarry at the guillotine, Anne Boleyn to executioners, and even *Das Weib des Pharaohs*' finale originally showed the lovers Theonis and Ramphis stoned to death followed by the Pharaoh collapsing on his throne. Where *Sumurun* toyed with the eponymous char-acter's beheading before her deliverance at the last moment, the history films almost necessitated such a finitude of life. The historicity of death made the display a modern reaction to the "loss of materiality and temporal experience" by highlighting "messages of matter," "scenes of erosion, and decay."[67] As light and shadow, even silent film had to show the destruction of sets, the death of human bodies, and the disruption of order to make the display a deeply felt duration.

With tragic ends to elongated historical narratives, the visual details of the films also offered a means of making time an experience associated with sensing one's own existence. All history is over and done by definition, yet if an audience can experience it—almost feel it—now, as it moves before them, then it cinematically extends into the here and now. The visual experi-ence keeps viewers in the present, but the suggestion of "haptic experience evokes the experience of a temporal continuum."[68] The linking of both pre-sent and past entwined temporalities as an experience of time. As one writer penned of *Dubarry*, the film commanded the past to "awake now, come into being and climb out of yesteryear."[69] As cinematic animation brought past to life in the present, the scenes of death and finite time brought present into a sense of past and finality.

While Lubitsch's other films (primarily comedies) produced during the same time period were generally 2000–4000 feet in length, his historical films ranged from 7500 to 9800 feet and they progressively lengthened.[70] The increased length, however, did not bring an increase in title cards. In fact, the opposite occurred.[71] The shift away from text-based history, thematized in *Dubarry* and occurring in Western cultures, was literally happening in the productions of Lubitsch, where history became increasingly a visual experience. The length of the historical productions also conveyed historicity by "writing" the subject matter's magnitude not just for posterity but on the audience's posterior, as Sobchack has phrased it.[72] The swelling length challenged physical bodies to sit through, endure, and experience duration on screen. In fact, the edited version of *Dubarry* as *Passion*, shown at its premiere in America, was dropped for the subsequent screening at Carnegie Hall, where it was announced that they would show all nine reels.[73] *Moving Picture World* wrote that *Dubarry*'s extended "length was hardly noticeable," since the film so powerfully held the "onlookers' interest."[74] Length was a double-edged sword. While it could inflict boredom, it also forced a bodily experience of temporality and allowed narrative extension.

As a representation of time in an extended narrative format, the history films of Lubitsch were even seen to inflect duration with significance. In a review for *Anne Boleyn*, the writer compared the film's sense of time with that of *Dubarry*. "Offhand one would say that 'Deception' was slower and heavier than 'Passion,' and isn't this the impression one would get from an actual comparison of the French Court life of Louis Bourbon and the English Court life of Henry Tudor?"[75] The "real authenticity of a historical production" was evidenced in the ability to create an appropriate sense of time—an authentic recreation of historically experienced time—to match the subject matter as an experience for a present audience.

With the increased length, directors were also able to include another type of temporal replication. By including elements of romance, tragedy, horror, and eroticism, the films could take viewers through the experience of varied temporal stimulations. Building on cinematically structured temporality, Williams has linked the genre conventions to psychoanalytic structures of fantasy, in order to describe how the temporality more generally attending the different types of attraction is enlisted. Like horror, the executions and bloody deaths in history films could signal the "too early," or shock, for which the audience was perhaps not prepared. Tragedy and melodrama could play off of a feeling of being "too late" (it might have been prevented). And finally, erotic attractions could get the audience to the titillating scene right "on time" (we fortunately caught it at the right moment).[76] Many history films, like *Dubarry*, combined all three in their slew of attractions. The structure of cinema at the time insisted the seated audience be taken through this roller coaster of temporal stimulation. This was part and parcel of a cinematic experience of history that could not, like a Sir Walter Scott novel, be bookmarked and put aside for a time.

History on Repeat

An extension of temporality was also created through repetition, an integral generic structure of historical epics. *Dubarry* repeated history, or made itself "historical" in its present moment, by "standing the test of time" for its revival two years later in New York,[77] creating the "German Invasion" into Hollywood, and intertextually through title cards. These intertitles function, like future voice-overs in sound films, to repeat the narrative in word before its visual enunciation, to teach audiences history from above. *Dubarry*, as *Passion* in America, opens with the title card "Great historic tragedies are vivid for a generation. Then against the back-drop of memory stand out the players, stars of a moment." The title cards link past to present retelling and extend that temporality through repetition, stamping modern historical time onto the past. The story of King Louis XV ruling France and Jeanne leaving country lanes for the court in her social ascension is told before the film visually begins and works to ensure historicity. The means by which historical time filters the cinematic experience is telling. Especially since "[h]istorical time is not simply an empty definition, but rather an entity, which alters along with history and from whose changing structure it is possible to deduce the shifting classification of experience and expectation," it is an important and formative feature.[78] In order to produce a modern mode of sensing historicity, the film turns on an embedded understanding of an already temporalized past.

Additionally, the fact that the film was immediately seen as historical (in its international appeal and ability to break the anti-German sentiment of the postwar market) further repeated history. Links between massive production and historic achievements accompanied many monumental, exotic, and historical films of the 1920s. The effort involved in creating such a scene of seeing the past confirmed the subject matter's merit as "worthy of repetition." This criterion is a foundational impetus for all history.

Using Ricoeur's articulation of repetition, as that "aspect of narratological form most responsive and responsible to our phenomenological sense of time as 'historical,'" Sobchack describes how repetition serves "to *extend* the temporal sense between the immediate and pre-reflective 'preoccupation' we have with time as 'now' and the deeply reflective sense we have of the transcendent unity of 'all times.'"[79] Repetition manufactures phenomenological relations between bodies and temporal horizons, by emphasizing the repeatability of the historical film's form. Additionally, as Robert Burgoyne has noted, the use of several genres for history telling works so well in film, since generic conventions are "organs of memory."[80] As a romance, tragedy, or melodrama history films could reach audiences viscerally and echo former uses of the genre, thus forging a bond between past and present.

Speaking of a Lubitsch historical film one reviewer commented, "and the special importance of this old and ever new story here is that the screen can tell it. Its psychological character is revealed through the medium of motion pictures."[81] The "old and ever new," or retold, repetitive aspect of history films bolsters the casting of stars and attention to pageantry that underlies the repetitive artifice and subjective nature of history as ultimately *histories*—stories to be told again and again with variation and diversity. There was no intolerable redundancy in the fact that a film titled *Madame Dubarry* had already been released by Fox Film in 1917. The repetition then, employed to stabilize and authenticate the "double exposure" of time, simultaneously haunts the endeavor as merely one iteration of all possibilities.

Repetition in the filmic medium also lends itself to a deep experience of temporality in that through persistence of vision, the past (literal profilmic event and sometimes historical representation) is always in the present tense.[82] This attribute of film makes history run again and again as a singular contingent, yet infinitely repeatable (profilmic) moment. This made history (as a recorded temporality) utterly representable. The resulting effect registers in the embodied experience of audiences, who sense the pastness of the images, which nevertheless live and move before them. Film created a history in purely the present tense. As the two temporalities coincide, the embodied experience of temporal extension has the capacity to spill over into reflective comprehension, but initially occurs as a carnal sensation. Audiences sense that the story of Dubarry is being repeated for good reason. It tautologically sells itself as "History" and important, because of its past iterations and present incarnation.

Page to Screen

The modern practice of history through sensual gazing described here does not lend itself to interpretation through the lens of strict historiography studies. There seems to be an insurmountable chasm between historiography proper and historical film. This is due primarily to the differing styles of historical objective and disciplinary practice. In terms of academic historiography, the films continue some notions of the "modern" regime of historicity since the end of the eighteenth century centered on the nation as the spatial framework for history and a linear, yet open-ended understanding of temporality. However, the popular level of historical culture and consciousness in many ways maintained elements of a premodern historicist mentality in its use and understanding of the past. Often, the cinematic past seems to restate its position as "being authoritative for the present in the form of practical exempla," which was characteristic of premodern historicity.[83]

In order to narrate these exemplary stories, films sided more closely with Sir Walter Scott than Ranke and as a popular form of history maintained the elements of dramatized narrative and experience. With the advent of nineteenth century *Historismus* and the consolidation of the academy, this traditional style of narrating the past did not disappear; it simply moved to other addresses—and film became one of those addresses.[84] Filmed history emerged in an entirely different network of demands and expectations than historicism; because of this, it is helpful to recognize how Lubitsch's films fit into a modern experience of the past, a cinematic regime of historicity, that coincided with advances in urbanity, technology, and capitalism.

Since "precisely what signifies temporal excess is not universal but culturally and historically determined," the historical experience of *Dubarry* should be seen as distinctly western and modern.[85] The culturally determined excess on film fit into discourses surrounding the experience of cinema and notions of absorption. Many witnesses to the rise of cinema saw its entangled relationship to modernity. In Hofmannsthal's 1921 article, "The Substitute for Dreams," cinema's images are said to be not only "strong" but to affect viewers "in their loins." The narrator concludes his remarks on cinema as a refuge for estranged victims of modernity by stating that it seems "the atmosphere of the cinema is the only one offering the people of our time—those who make up the masses—an immediate and unrestrained relation to an enormous (even if oddly presented) cultural heritage."[86]

The immediacy of flickering films was seen already by Strobl in 1911 to be the "perfect expression of [the] time. Its quick, distracted tempo correspond[ed] to the nervousness" of modern life. The absence of words was only further testament to the spirit of the times, in which modern life had supplanted the "old contemplativeness" with a "constant presence of mind."[87] Two decades before Benjamin would describe audiences' shift in attention, from concentration to absorption in distraction,[88] the phenomenon was already ripe for examination. Strobl also noted that the "spectator ha[d] a sense for splendid processions, displays of military pomp and royal encounters; he enjoys being impressed … laughing … to be titillated, and in the end he longs for the noble surge of moving emotions."[89] In order to create historical experience for modern subjects, film proliferated images of the past that sutured historicity with "noble surges." The historical representations in film should, therefore, be considered as experiences just as much as narratives.

Distinct from historiographic narratives, historical films also increasingly began to be packaged in a fitting architectural experience. Like the binding of a history book, the proliferation of movie "palaces" in the 1920s shaped the opening and closing of the experience of the film. Although cinema palaces began to flourish in the early 1920s, "[i]t was only in Weimar

Germany that the movie palace first emerged as a site that reached far beyond the nineteenth-century stylistic pastiches of world's fair, vaudeville, and stage theater."[90] Appropriately, *Dubarry*'s premiere marked the reopening of the UFA-Palast am Zoo as the "most beautiful theater in Germany so far." Several photographs of the interior were included in the cursory report of the new theater in the *Illustrierte Filmwoche*.[91] The Palast was praised for its visibility from any seat in the house and the combinations of gold with purple and green lent the interior a lavish royal touch.[92] The new palace, like the dressing up of theater ushers at *Dubarry*'s premiere in America, evidenced how much the location of the projection itself shaped the bodily experience of history on film. The literally felt textures and architecture of the cinema were not divorced from the spectatorial enterprise.

As paying viewers, audiences wanted spectacle as a return on their investment. In postwar European countries, as well as America, history signified on screen appeared in the singular spectacle and excessive existence of historical material that defied modern consumer culture while attesting to the same through its own production. The construction and destruction of sets and figures spoke to the mobilization of massive historical workforces. This was a deep materiality that is abandoned in today's disaster movies (and epics), which employ computer-generated images.[93] The singularity of dress and set design was born from the same remarkable workforce of set designers and costumers, yet signaled a certain uniqueness of the historical period.

For many historical films, like *Dubarry*, the spectacle of handiwork on screen resonated with a nostalgia for earlier modes of production. Like the arts and crafts movement that swept the continent in the late nineteenth century, historical film projects could create handmade trinkets and worlds. Yet, a modern technology of reproduction was required to make these artworks available for international consumption.[94] All the historical and authentic details were set against the present, while simultaneously attesting to the consumer culture's capacity to produce and visually consume such detail on display. The film's exhibitionism worked culturally to viscerally bombard viewers with signifiers of the past in terms of the present's modes of production and consumption. The effort (especially when time equals money) put into creating the mise-en-scène seemed to demand documentation through recording it all onto celluloid—effectively archiving a history of capitalism.

All these conventions speak to the specificity of the medium to generate carnal historical experience for modern subjects. However, Lubitsch's so-called "touch" also colored the reception of *Madame Dubarry*. One such use of his idiosyncratic style is illustrated in *Dubarry*'s play with vision. Like many other such instances, a court official sees the scene mentioned earlier (of the king placing the text in Jeanne's breast) through a keyhole.

This voyeuristic royal official not only mimics the spectator's relationship to history on screen, but also affirms that history is something "emphatically 'to be looked at.'"[95] The process of world audiences taking history onto their persons through sensory experience is bound up with visual consumption. This attention to vision also has direct consequences for the phenomenological experience of history on film. This is once again a repetition—a multiplication of what might be pigeonholed as merely self-reflexive cinema. However, when this is visually emphasized and linked with historical representation, the film marries Sobchack's "objective seeing subjective seeing" with Ankersmit's "subjective historical experience."[96] The film doubles the gaze and takes the audience through historical spaces to see and cross-modally smell and feel the meticulous detail. *Madame Dubarry*, then, served to literalize the craft of the historian: historical visualization.

In making space for the cultural work of softer history and focusing on experience, instead of instrumentalized narratives, Lubitsch emerges as something of an international cinematic historian. His ability to write history onto the bodies of audiences overcame the temporal frame between past and present, by putting it to productive use. In carnal ways, *Dubarry* created a valid experience of history made possible because of the filmic medium's blizzard surface qualities, which worked on a neglected, yet significant sensory level. It also evaded a historicist avalanche of facts and footnotes that would sublimate bodily experience to cognition. Viewing Lubitsch's film in this theoretically embodied light, between the two historiographical blizzards, reveals an early moment in the development of the cinematic sense of history. This sense, abounding with sensation, worked against "scientific knowledge" of the past, which had "shift[ed] the center of gravity of experience, so that we unlearned how to see, hear, and generally speaking, feel."[97] A new sense of history was ushered in with the advent of film and solidified with feature historical film conventions, viewing practices, and durations. This phenomenological experience would solicit varied responses. Politically, pedagogically, and professionally, the experience of history on film required careful attention for those concerned with the power of the past in present.

Notes

1 Egon Friedell, "Dubarry," *Weltbühne* 17, March 10, 1921, 277.
2 In 1936, Erwin Panofsky remembered the queen's head "actually com[ing] off" and linked this effect to "a primordial instinct for bloodshed and cruelty." See Panofsky, "Style and Medium in the Motion Pictures," in *Film Theory and Criticism; Introductory Readings*, eds. Gerald Mast and Marshall Cohen (New York, NY: Oxford University Press, 1974), 153.

3 Siegfried Kracauer used the film to show, "as the few meters of celluloid film prove, the inclination toward terror has ever been inherent in film art" since cinema has again and again "visualized events that evoke horror." See Kracauer, "Das Grauen im Film," in *Werke 6.3: Kleine Schriften zum Film 1932–1961*, eds. Inka Mülder-Bach, Mirjam Wenzel, and Sabine Biebl (Frankfurt: Suhrkamp, 2004), 312–13.

4 Daniel Arasse traces these and further parallels between portrait photography and the guillotine in, *The Guillotine and the Terror* (London: Lane, 1989), 139. I am gratefully indebted to Gertrud Koch for alerting me to this source.

5 Ibid., 140.

6 Leopold von Ranke, *Sämtliche Werke*, 54 vols. (Leipzig: Duncker & Humblot, 1875–1890), xv.103. See Stuart Macintyre, Juan Maiguashca, and Attila Pók, *The Oxford History of Historical Writing: Volume 4: 1800–1945* (Oxford: Oxford University Press, 2011), 42.

7 Siegfried Kracauer, *Theory of Film: The Redemption of Physical Reality* (Princeton, NJ: Princeton University Press, 1997), xvii.

8 Siegfried Kracauer, *From Caligari to Hitler: A Psychological History of the German Film* (Princeton, NJ: Princeton University Press, 1947), 52.

9 Christian Keathley, *Cinephilia and History, or, the Wind in the Trees* (Bloomington: Indiana University Press, 2006), 9.

10 The affective and imagistic qualities of film are some of the "soft" factors providing historians so much difficulty. See Günter Riederer, "Film und Geschichtswissenschaft," in *Visual History*, ed. Gerhard Paul (Germany: Vandenhoeck & Ruprecht, 2006), 102.

11 Paul Ricoeur, *Memory, History, Forgetting*, trans. Kathleen Blamey and David Pellauer, 1st ed. (Chicago: University of Chicago Press, 2004), 120.

12 Ibid., 498.

13 Siegfried Kracauer and Paul Oskar Kristeller, *History: The Last Things Before the Last* (Princeton, NJ: M. Wiener, 1995), 84.

14 Siegfried Kracauer, "Photography" in *The Mass Ornament: Weimar Essays* (Cambridge, MA: Harvard University Press, 1995), 58.

15 Quoted in Frank Ankersmit, *Sublime Historical Experience* (Stanford, CA: Stanford University Press, 2005), 11.

16 F. R. Ankersmit, *History and Tropology: The Rise and Fall of Metaphor* (Berkeley, CA: University of California Press, 1994), 148–49.

17 Kerwin Lee Klein, "On the Emergence of Memory in Historical Discourse," *Representations* 69 (Winter 2000): 127.

18 Kracauer, "Photography," 51.

19 Ankersmit, *Sublime Historical Experience*, 265.

20 For earlier examples of film shaping the structure of historical imagination, see Chapter 4.

21 Kracauer, *Theory of Film*, 158.

22 Miriam Bratu Hansen, *Cinema and Experience: Siegfried Kracauer, Walter Benjamin, and Theodor W. Adorno* (Berkeley, CA: University of California Press, 2011), 268.

23 For sustained "textural" analysis of film, see Jennifer Barker, *The Tactile Eye: Touch and the Cinematic Experience* (Berkeley, CA: University of California Press, 2009).

24 Vivan Sobchack, *Carnal Thoughts: Embodiment and Moving Image Culture* (Berkeley, CA: University of California Press, 2004), 76.

25 Carlo Mierendorff, "If I Only Had the Movies!!" in *The Promise of Cinema: German Film Theory 1907–1933*, eds. Anton Kaes, Michael Cowan, and Nicholas Baer (Berkeley, CA: University of California Press, 2016), 428.

26 Giacomo Rizzolatti and Corrado Sinigaglia, *Mirrors in the Brain: How Our Minds Share Actions, Emotions, and Experience* (Oxford: Oxford University Press, 2008).

27 Albert Hellwig, "Illusions and Hallucinations during Cinematographic Projections," in *The Promise of Cinema*, eds. Anton Kaes, Nicholas Baer, and Michael Cowan (Berkeley, CA: University of California Press, 2016), 46.

28 Linda Williams, "Film Bodies: Gender, Genre, and Excess," *Film Quarterly* 44, no. 4 (July 1991): 2–13.

29 Marc Silberman, *German Cinema: Texts in Context* (Detroit, MI: Wayne State University Press, 1995), 7.

30 Walter Benjamin, *Arcades Project*, trans. Howard Eiland and Kevin McLaughlin (Cambridge, MA: Belknap Press, 1999), (N11, 4), 476.

31 Vivian Sobchack, "'Surge and Splendor': A Phenomenology of the Hollywood Historical Epic," *Representations* 29 (Winter 1990): 26.

32 Georg Lukacs, *The Historical Novel* (London: Merlin Press, 1962), 23.

33 Reinhart Koselleck also described the "forcible experience of the French Revolution, which seemed to outstrip all previous experience" as part of the larger shift in temporalized history. Reinhart Koselleck and Keith Tribe, *Futures Past: On the Semantics of Historical Time* (New York, NY: Columbia University Press, 1985), 38.

34 Friedell, "Dubarry," 278.

35 Hansen, *Cinema and Experience*, 259.

36 Philip Rosen, *Change Mummified: Cinema, Historicity, Theory* (Minneapolis, MN: University of Minnesota Press, 2001), 149.

37 Scott Eyman, *Ernst Lubitsch: Laughter in Paradise* (Baltimore, MD: Johns Hopkins University Press, 2000), 60–61.

38 Similarly, "original music written by Anne Boleyn and Henry VIII was dug out of the forgotten archives" for Lubitsch's next film *Deception* (*Anne Boleyn*, 1920). See Hugo Rosenfeld, "Music and Motion Pictures," *Annals of the American Academy of Political and Social Science. The Motion Picture in Its Economic and Social Aspects* 128 (November, 1926): 60.

39 Silberman, *German Cinema*, 7.

40 Ibid., 156.

41 Thomas Elsaesser, *Weimar Cinema and After: Germany's Historical Imaginary* (London: Routledge, 2000), 197.

42 Ankersmit, *Sublime Historical Experience*, xiv–xv.

43 Ibid., 10.

44 Ibid., 233.

45 Ludmilla Jordanova, *History in Practice* (London: Routledge, 2000), 153.

46 Miriam Hansen even connects Griffith's use of elephants to his viewing of *Cabiria*, in *Babel and Babylon: Spectatorship in American Silent Film* (Cambridge, MA: Harvard University Press, 1991), 176–77.

47 Quoted in Joseph Garncarz, "The Star System in Weimar Cinema," in *The Many Faces of Weimar Cinema: Rediscovering Germany's Filmic Legacy*, ed. Christian Rogowski (Rochester, NY: Camden House, 2010), 120.

48 Mila Ganeva, *Women in Weimar Fashion: Discourses and Displays in German Culture, 1918–1933* (Rochester, NY: Camden House, 2008), 113–50.

49 Robert Rosenstone, *Visions of the Past: The Challenge of Film to Our Idea of History* (Cambridge, MA: Harvard University Press, 1995), 59.

50 Ganeva, *Women in Weimar Fashion*, 291, 300.
51 This was also a consequence of Sigmund Lindauer's patenting of the modern brassiere in Germany in 1914.
52 *LA Times*, June 4, 1921, 11.
53 Cover of *Vogue* as advertised in *The New York Times*, May 5, 1921, 4.
54 Daniel Delis Hill, *As Seen in Vogue: A Century of American Fashion in Advertising* (Lubbock, TX: Texas Tech University Press, 2007), 36.
55 Ibid., 54.
56 Juhani Pallasmaa, "Hapticity and Time: Notes on Fragile Architecture," *Architectural Review* 207, no. 1239 (May 2000): 323.
57 Sobchack, "'Surge and Splendor,'" 36.
58 Elsaesser, *Weimar Cinema and After*, 197.
59 Quoted in Kracauer, *From Caligari to Hitler*, 55.
60 "The Screen," *New York Times*, December 13, 1920, 21.
61 Wilhelm Dilthey, Rudolf A. Makkreel, and Frithjof Rodi, *Hermeneutics and the Study of History* (Princeton, NJ: Princeton University Press, 1996), 236.
62 Pallasmaa, "Hapticity and Time," 331.
63 Ankersmit, *History and Tropology*, 141.
64 "Lubitsch-Negri Abend," *Lichtbild Bühne* 38, September 20, 1919.
65 See Kathrin Maurer, *Discursive Interaction: Literary Realism and Academic Historiography in Nineteenth-Century Germany* (Heidelberg: Synchron, 2006).
66 Kracauer, *From Caligari to Hitler*, 51.
67 Pallasmaa, "Hapticity and Time," 325.
68 Ibid., 324.
69 Herbert Lulenberg, "Festspruch zur Eröffnung des UFA-Palastes am Zoo mit dem Film Madame Dubarry," *Illustrierte Filmwoche* 39, 1919.
70 Lengths furnished through quotation of miscellaneous sources compiled in Robert L. Carringer and Barry Sabath, *Ernst Lubitsch: A Guide to References and Resources* (Boston, MA: G. K. Hall, 1978).
71 "Screen: Soundless Oratory" *New York Times*, February 19, 1922, 71. See also Chapter 2.
72 Sobchack, "'Surge and Splendor,'" 38.
73 *Moving Picture World*, February 5, 1921, 678.
74 Ibid.
75 "Brought into Focus," *New York Times*. April 24, 1921, X2.
76 Williams, "Film Bodies," 11.
77 *The New York Times*, June 26th 1923, 14.
78 Koselleck and Tribe, *Futures Past*, 259.
79 Sobchack, "'Surge and Splendor,'" 38.
80 Burgoyne, *The Epic Film*, 1.
81 "Screen," *New York Times*, March 5, 1922, 80.
82 Mary Anne Doan, *The Emergence of Cinematic Time: Modernity, Contingency, the Archive* (Cambridge, MA: Harvard University Press, 2002), 10.
83 Chris Lorenz, "Unstuck in Time. Or: The Sudden Presence of the Past," in *Performing the Past: Memory, History, and Identity in Modern Europe*, ed. Karin Tilmans (Amsterdam: Amsterdam University Press, 2010), 75.
84 Elaine Tennant, "Traditional Historiography in Early Modern Germany," in *Poetics and Reformations: Histories and Reformations*, eds. Christopher Ocker, Michael Rinty, Peter Starenko, and Peter Wallace (Leiden: Brill, 2007), 195.
85 Sobchack, "'Surge and Splendor,'" 29.

86 Hugo von Hofmannsthal, "A Substitute for Dreams," in *The Promise of Cinema*, ed. Anton Kaes, Nicholas Baer, Michael Cowan (Berkeley, CA: University of California Press, 2016), 386.

87 Karl Hans Strobl, "The Cinematographer," in *The Promise of Cinema*, eds. Anton Kaes, Nicholas Baer, Michael Cowan (Berkeley, CA: University of California Press, 2016), 26–27.

88 Walter Benjamin, "The Work of Art in the Age of Mechanical Reproducibility," *Selected Writings*, vol. 3, (Cambridge: Harvard University Press, 2002), 119.

89 Strobl, "The Cinematographer," 26.

90 Janet Ward, *Weimar Surfaces: Urban Visual Culture in 1920s Germany* (Berkeley, CA: University of California Press, 2001), 178.

91 Lulenberg, *Illustrierte Filmwoche*, 41.

92 Sabine Hake, *Passions and Deceptions: The Early Films of Ernst Lubitsch* (Princeton, NJ: Princeton University Press, 1992), 119.

93 This recognition is from Vivian Sobchack in "Vivian Sobchack in Conversation with Scott Bukatman," *E-media Studies* 2 (2009).

94 I am indebted to Gertrud Koch for this connection.

95 Sobchack, "'Surge and Splendor,'" 37.

96 Sobchack, *Carnal Thoughts*, 150.

97 Maurice Merleau-Ponty, *Phenomenology of Perception*, trans. Colin Smith (London: Routledge, 1962), 229.

2 Entangling Histories

"The development of the film drama has long since blasted beyond what had appeared to be its natural limits (*Grenzen*)."

—Oscar Geller, 1922[1]

The experience of cinematic history had potential to move people. It could possibly bring nations of bodies together into shared historical experiences. In May of 1922, American film director D. W. Griffith traveled to Europe, motivated by a deep faith in this capacity of the medium. His aim abroad was to confer with several influential leaders and historians to rally support for his incredibly ambitious, "film peace project."[2] The project Griffith had proposed entailed, "a chronological history of every country" and required international cooperation in its "promot[ion of] peace." When describing the arduous and costly peace project Griffith said, "the foremost historians of every country will collaborate in preparing the scenario." The historical series—translating national histories into the "universal language" of silent film—would be a "stupendous lesson and propaganda against war," by turning history into lessons for the present, in a visual, and therefore democratized form.[3] Unfortunately for Griffith, the project never fully materialized.

Yet, by traversing national borders and pushing the limits of the genre, Griffith's intentions capture what was at stake for historical film in the post-war world. His was a present overflowing with the utopian potential of silent film as an international force for peace and a cinematic counterpart to the League of Nations. Film could use history to bring bodies, even international ones, together and instruct them in progressive and moving ways. And Griffith was not alone in this conviction. The sentiment was felt internationally, since the present of 1922, set in the shadow of the horrific Great War, seemed to require such connective world projects.

In some senses, Griffith's idea was already underway as nations and ambitious directors entered the international market with widely screened historical films. Ernst Lubitsch, who was even nicknamed the "European Griffith," most prominently achieved the effect.[4] Lubitsch brought the German film industry into the realm of history filmmaking explicitly for international audiences. While Lubitsch's films were easily the most popular, they appeared alongside dozens of other historical features. In fact, the period from 1919 to 1924 still remains the most prolific for the genre of history films in Germany and historians have had difficulty accounting for this short-lived boom.

Both Griffith's and Lubitsch's historical films have traditionally been written off as escapist fluff or portrayed as nationalist products, continuing the war on the film front. However, these characterizations neglect the films' cultural force and perpetuate a distorted view of their reception. By treating additional sources from the films' *international* reception and recognizing how they fit into conceptions of world projects aimed at peace, I argue that the films utilized and shared world history as connective tissue between nations. In order to tease out the entanglement and the social energy of silent historical films, in the wake of the First World War, this chapter focuses on limits, borders, and traffic, as symptomatically prevalent themes of relations between international bodies. For these borders were the very constructions that required crossing in order to reach and homogenize diverse bodies, both national and biological.

Where the German word "Grenze" can mean both limit and border, its multiple translations here will necessarily be reduced to one or the other. However, in both senses, the distinct presence of the concept of pushing limits appears within the films themselves as well as the accompanying discourse in film reviews and journalism. As mentioned in the last chapter, attention to the generic use of excess and spectacle reveals the monumental manner, in which Lubitsch's silent historical films reach beyond themselves visually. The spectacular display of *mis-en-scène* stretches beyond the frame and stimulates "container schemata" in the spectator as a primary method for comprehending the action.[5] This cognitive semiotic means of understanding involves the embodied viewer's completion, or continuation, of the images on screen beyond the frame—into offscreen space. Since the historical films employed pageantry and excessive material display across the frame, they came to function through container models of thought that echoed conceptions of national confinement and the postwar reconstitution of borders. In other words, Lubitsch's films made history reach beyond limits and borders, including national ones.

Using history in cinema to traverse borders spoke to a present, in which conceptions of national borders were ubiquitous and at times, ambiguous. At the end of the war, entire nations were reorganized into a cartography reflecting a "new world order." The pressing political reality of borders and international relations was refracted through the limits of the history

genre like light through a prism. While this effect comprised the proliferation of spectacle and the excess of conceived limits of representation and
reality effects, cinematically it brought audiences across borders and into
connection.

The unity of a common cinematic past was constructed through a distinct
play with temporality. By treating other national histories and distant periods
(pasts), for decidedly international bodies of spectators (present/presence),
the limits of the content (lavish displays) and reception (box office sales)
were also pushed. To be an effective world project, the limits had to be
pushed to ensure an *experience*. Stories, actors, lighting, stunts, and even
movie palaces had to reach new heights. All this served to evoke the superlative language that became so common in the marketing and reviewing
of historical films.[6] It was here, in cinema's third machine of film criticism
that the play with limits surfaced on a grammatical level in the discourse
surrounding history films.[7] The prestige of historical representation, along
with the appeal of spectacle and period detail, made history emphatically *for*
international and embodied viewing subjects. Because the genre itself was
so involved with notions of transcending borders and limits, it also served
as a condensing point for (inter)national understanding. Recognizing the
genre's transnational nature not only illuminates Griffith's zealous history
project and the success of Lubitsch's history films abroad, but also helps to
bring the tension between imperial/nationalistic mentalities and burgeoning
international conceptions of a new world order into relief.

A Common Past

The concept of overcoming divides through an ostensibly universal language depended on sematic borrowings from a variety of sources spanning
from "the Bible, Protestant millennialism, the French Encyclopedists, contemporary movements such as Esperanto and Progressive reformism," as
well as postwar pacifism.[8] Silent film, as an intensely visual medium, fit well
into such conceptions.[9] Especially since a dominant style of cinema was still
being developed, film lent itself to the image of a universal language under
construction. However, it was not only the transnational medium of film
that was so democratizing and inclusive. Historical material itself seemed to
have a melting-pot effect of bringing audiences together into a relationship
with what was increasingly a common past.

"We can't change the past, but we can apply its lessons toward the development of a better future," stated Richard Coudenhove-Kalergi in his 1923
call for pan-European unity.[10] Like Griffith's historical cinema, pan-Europe-
anism's tendentious turn to the past was another symptom of a larger inclination for "world projects." Making sense of a postwar world seemed to

necessitate reexplanation or even reorganization. The cooperation and world projects so common before the breakout of the First World War arose once more.[11] In the realm of history, Oswald Spengler's philosophical means of world making/explaining in *The Decline of the West* was published alongside Wells' *Outline of History*.[12] Both projects seemed to offer "everything one needs to know" and conceptualized history on a grand scale.

The sentiment was echoed across nations with efforts to rewrite history textbooks after the war. German postwar history schoolbooks made the emphatic point to correct the "old style" of writing about Germany in an "isolated" way that had included only a "tacked-on glance at the other nations."[13] The new internationalism went against the grain of jingoist or ethnocentric historiography. In a didactic effort for peace, for instance, with the presentation of wars "their frightfulness was to be emphasized."[14] The deliberate demonizing of military history fit within a pacifist trend and perceived notions of guilt after the war.[15] German pedagogue Herr von Gerlach confidently proclaimed, "We are reconstructing our school textbooks. We are going to teach our school children history without filling them with the thirst for victory over other people."[16] The new textbooks left out the "vainglory of German arms" and after comparing these with "an old-style history, full of flamboyant war stuff," American journalist Freeman Tilden found the newer text to be a "milestone on the way to world peace." This historiographic shift entailed a repositioning of the nation and past within an intimately woven nexus of other nations. The wider international viewpoint was meant to foster real-world understanding. In this view, the past was at once a world project and an informational bridge. It was supposed to, as Griffith surmised, unite peoples of the present and become usable in the effort to ensure peace.

Along with modified presentations of history in classrooms, filmed histories in cinemas shaped a new generational historical culture. As an international phenomenon, history put on film had medium-specific consequences that were widespread. Because historical film helped to "exteriorize memory," it made versions of the past more easily shared and trafficked.[17] With the increased flow of historical projections, otherwise distinct audiences were connected in their ability to experience common pasts as something akin to "prosthetic memories."[18] As memories, or subjective versions of the past available for consumption and mental incorporation, the films staged historical imagination in communal settings. The ability to view, experience, and even identify with myriad images was coupled with the flow and entanglement of transnational historical representations, forever changing a mass understanding and relationship to history. As a new media network, these popular silent films "articulated, multiplied, and globalized a particular historical experience" of history itself.[19] They have often been dismissed as hollow escapism after a brutal war or in reaction to new-found freedom.[20] But historical films challenged traditional notions of history and raised questions of international connections within and beyond Germany. They created a common and entangled past through an economically and culturally entangled present, by focusing on monumental display for embodied viewers.

Cinematic Historians

Griffith had good reason to return to the volatile power of history on film in order to connect nations in peace. His previous hits, *The Birth of a Nation* (1915) and *Intolerance* (1916), had both been box office successes at home as well as abroad, solidifying the appeal of history on film. Just before his ambitious trip to Europe, Griffith had revisited the history genre with the French Revolutionary story, *Orphans of the Storm* (1921); consequently, world history was likely on his mind.[21] Griffith might also have harbored a personal interest in creating some epic historical project as a means of recuperating his directorial stature in the face of the rising German filmmaker Ernst Lubitsch, who had gradually garnered more praise and sales than Griffith. Especially since Griffith seems to have envisioned himself as the director to bring the world history scenario to life on screen, the stupendous peace project would surely catapult his name back into the limelight. However, at the time of Griffith's departure, it was Lubitsch who was enjoying that very limelight with his meticulously constructed historical dramas.

Although Lubitsch is more often remembered for his comedies, from the perspective of silent historical film and Weimar Germany's entry into this transnational genre his work was second to none. Lubitsch rose to fame in Berlin and his films traveled exceedingly well in the often-hostile climate of the postwar market. Indeed, Griffith had already responded to Lubitsch's success by rereleasing *The Birth of a Nation*, in an unsuccessful effort to outgross Lubitsch's first international historical hit, *Passion* (1920). Griffith reportedly canceled his subscription to *Variety* after the magazine charted the success of *Passion*, which had "played more performances and attracted larger audiences" than *Birth*.[22] Although words of mutual admiration were voiced, the relationship between Griffith and Lubitsch took place primarily through their films. In an era that was consuming history through spectacular films, Griffith and Lubitsch were at the helm of collective memory making with their intertextual films. Griffith helped forge the narrative editing style assumed most conducive for embodied audiences to comprehend. Lubitsch created visual display that evoked psychological and carnal responses (usually laughter or even arousal). Even with individual approaches to filmmaking, the two cinematic historians helped shape the conception of the past into a visual and, above all, international experience.

The Philadelphia premiere of Lubitsch's first historical film turned international hit, *Dubarry* as *Passion*, further emphasized the film's translation of history into an experience. It involved a meticulously decorated theater interior and ushers dressed for the event in "Louis XV court costumes." Audience members sat among the excessive pageantry, crowding the ballroom floor "almost to the point of suffocation to see the most talked of motion picture production in years."[23] This Philadelphia opening, along with several New Jersey showings, functioned as a precursor that helped define the magnitude of the film before its screening in New York.[24] The opulent marketing signaled the arrival of German film into the international body and flow of historical epics.

For Lubitsch and his producer, Paul Davidson, arrival was not enough. In an effort to continue the newfound international success, they revisited the genre with *Anna Boleyn* in 1921. Before it was released in America as *Deception* and in order to prime the marketing pump, German President Friedrich Ebert visited the set and was photographed with the cast and director.[25] With the publicity and box office success surrounding *Passion* and *Deception*, *The Loves of Pharaoh* seemed a shoo-in and capped the three major historical works directed by Lubitsch.

The Loves of Pharaoh was mostly well received abroad and exhibited the internationality of silent film, as a material and conceptual connecting force between nations, more than any prior Lubitsch creation. This was a result of Lubitsch's careful attention to international filmmaking on formal and narrative levels. Like Griffith, Lubitsch saw film as intrinsically international. He also demanded that history was not to be monopolized by parochial nationalism, but that world history belonged to the entire world. He stated that his films were made so that "everyone—regardless of linguistic and political borders—could understand. Every good film is by nature international." Lubitsch could actualize the statement by addressing the carnality of viewers, which effectively transcended cultural divides. He went so far as to afford film a privileged status above national borders and political conditions. Lubitsch was convinced that "no politics [could] stop the triumphal march of a perfect work of film art."[26] In realization of his views, *The Loves of Pharaoh* not only premiered on American soil, but diegetically depicted the Ethiopian King Samlak forging a treaty with the Egyptian Pharaoh Amenes.

As a cautionary tale, the plot reveals the tragedy of personal vice over political relations. Beyond the explicit rendition of international relations (gone awry), the film also follows the fate of a Greek slave to an Ethiopian queen after her arrival in Egypt. This narrative hook rivals the international appeal of *Passion*'s depiction of commoner Jeanne Vaubenier's social ascension from humble millinery to the royal court and Anne Boleyn's rise to becoming crowned queen of England. In such ways, Lubitsch's historical films tended to foreground the seemingly universal interest in the historical agency of figures in varied cultural, class, and national contexts.

Scholars, like Peter Burgoyne, have argued that late twentieth- and early twenty-first-century epic films exhibit just such a multicultural or transnational dimension in order for producers to broaden the films' appeal and to "recoup their investment."[27] However, historical epics of the silent era already employed a transnational strategy. Because the films and directors worked within the increased construction of international viewing subjects, confining our understanding of the films to national cinemas or even mere expressions of nationalism is much too limiting. While traditional accounts of French impressionism, German expressionism, and Soviet montage provide important insights into the history of cinema and nationalism between the wars, their construction also tends to obscure the cross-fertilization of cinema in production and reception. The categories often edit out the influence and reaction between "national" cinemas and the composition of what were overwhelmingly *international* genres made for travel.

In other words, as Thomas Saunders put it, "it is scarcely possible to understand German cinema in this period apart from its steady dialogue, both friendly and hostile, with Hollywood."[28] Of course, the same could be said of other national styles, which equally informed the production of many German films. With all this mutual influence, by the Weimar period, "popular cinema had developed a transnational stock of narrative and visual tropes."[29] Diverse national directors and genres could employ this visual lexicon for wide international audiences. With this in mind, looking back on "national" cinemas we might now, in the early twenty-first-century, see just how "transnational the world has always been, even in the high days when the nation state bounded and bundled most social processes."[30] This transnational lens is appropriate in that notions of the potential or threat of Americanism and cosmopolitanism suffused postwar Germany. The spirit of internationalism was a hallmark of Weimar culture and this was seen by contemporary viewers to be explicitly evidenced in historical films.[31] Lubitsch's blockbuster history films were no exception.

All three films serve as narratives of travel and crossings and each explores social (im)mobility and national conflict for a wide audience demographic. Because they address universal bodies more than specific countries, it is little surprise that the films often gesture toward global connections. In setting up this thematic each film begins with explicit reference to international commerce and travel.

The third shot in *Passion* is a unique point of view (POV) from a female customer browsing the milliner's shop where Jeanne works. The POV shot reveals an advertisement for the "most beautiful flowers from Italy," which have recently arrived in France. This seemingly trivial reference subtly places the viewing subject (in the theater as well as the character in the film) in France by way of relationship to another space, namely, Italy. While the shot conjures up permeable national borders, the lavish flowers between Jeanne's fingers serve as conspicuous corroboration. Along with period costumes, such details temporally locate the audience in the thick of historical happenings and between nations. Jeanne's handling of the flowers also engages the very material texture of the representation on screen. The scene visualizes and literalizes *feeling* the mediated connection between the two national locations.

A similar effect initiates Lubitsch's next historical film. An impressive exterior shot lends the opening of *Deception* the gravitas of history through blockbuster production value. The film opens with a superbly staged rocking shot of a vast ocean accented with a single ship. The first stabilizing moment is the initial intertitle stating "on the journey from France to England." This title card of relief not only stills the frame but also locates the motion in reference to national origins and destinations. That is, the audience primarily identifies with the movement of the camera but understands this motion to have purpose and direction between national borders. The film also focuses on and frames bodily sensation (now of rocking), in order to enact the transportation of audience members between just such borders.

And finally, in the beginning of *The Loves of Pharaoh*, King Samlak arrives from Ethiopia. The king greets the Pharaoh of Egypt and offers him treasures, along with his daughter, in an effort to unite the two nations. This immediate invasion of the frame from another nation calls on the spectator to construct ancient Egypt in relation to Ethiopia. Like the other two films, *Pharaoh* locates the action geographically through reference to other nations, which stand in connection through commerce and travel. The narrative networks implicate and recreate the interconnectedness of trafficked reels of historical films, traveling directors, and international locations of reception. In the films, as in intertwined film industries, it becomes impossible to ignore other nations even in the representation of otherwise enclosed national pasts. Internationality is both felt and conceptualized across formal, national, and imagined borders.

The travel of celluloid, style, and images was also embodied in Griffith, Lubitsch, Abel Gance, and others who saw each other's work, traveled between nations and created films within a remarkably international genre.[32] This produced a profound intertextual and international connection of directors, audiences, and governments—an entangled internationality of silent film that shaped an entangled conception of the past. Film industries manufactured history as an international affair on the popular level of the historical culture. The common sense of what is historical, or historicity, was informed by this increasingly connected world film culture.

History for Export

The genre of the historical film has traditionally been informed by a central paradox in both production and reception. On the one hand, the messages embedded in these films are generally understood as national narratives of "the birth of a nation, the emergence of a people, [or] the fulfillment of a heroic destiny." On the other hand, the films possess a long history of being an "international, global narrative apparatus not bound by nation or ethnicity."[33] Lubitsch deftly exploited this dual nature. Despite their overt exhibitionism, the history films produced by Lubitsch began in relative isolation. Like *The Cabinet of Dr. Caligari* (1919), *Passion* was reportedly made "without any consideration for the foreign market."[34] Whether this lack of conscious desire for export is true or not, Germany was still under a ban on foreign importation, which greatly reduced the amount and variety of films available to Lubitsch. It is unclear how familiar he would have been with American tastes even if he had deliberately catered to other national markets. However, before American film came to dominate the German market, Lubitsch had other models available to him.

Shortly before the war, the Italian spectacles of *Quo Vadis?* (1913) and *Cabiria* (1914) created the blueprint for epic historical filmmaking and both acquired wide international praise, thereby setting the standard. An American review of *Cabiria* already placed it with the "greatest classics" of film, which included Italy's other historical feature, *The Fall of Troy*, from 1910. Without having seen Griffith's reaction to the Italian spectacles in *Judith of Bethulia* (1914), *Birth of a Nation* (1915) and *Intolerance* (1916), Lubitsch began primarily from the tradition of German, Swedish, and Italian filmmaking.

Only after the major Germany film corporation Universum-Film AG (UFA) began to contractually import previously released American films (of the war period) in 1919 and the foreign importation ban was lifted, in December of 1920, did the German film industry begin to become increasingly informed by American taste.[35] This represented an important shift from the wartime xenophobia aimed against "all things foreign, especially [...] foreign films."[36] The prewar Italian epics had "open[ed] the eyes of the world" and "creat[ed] new records" by pressing the classical theme and spectacle "to the limit."[37] Already with *Quo Vadis?* German critic Kurt Pinthus noted, "precisely this film shows the potential of cinema, as well as its limits." By presenting an unprecedented display of detail and destruction, the film showed that cinema "can make the impossible possible."[38] American critic James McQuade echoed Pinthus' glowing review by conceding that "the mere use of superlatives" would be inadequate and found the film to have "the most impressive spectacles ever pictured."[39] The exceptional quality of spectacular display pushed the medium in order to find limits and this created "historical" embodied experience for international audiences and critics. This internationality through spectacle became the guiding formula for cinematic historical representation.

What was previously "film as internal propaganda" during the war became "film as ambassador abroad."[40] For postwar Germany, this was first evident with Joe May's epic trilogy *Veritas Vincit* (1918/1919). It was May's display of historical periods, as Oskar Kalbus noted, that "drew the attention of the entire world to the German Film industry for the first time."[41] Although the veracity of this statement is in question, especially since Siegfried Kracauer would call the film a "nonentity," the real significance lies in the conception of an epic form of historical filmmaking that would command attention.[42] The "first time" unprecedented nature of epics was a staple description that would continue alongside hyperbole (such as "the *entire* world" of reception). Blockbuster films bridged borders and reached any *body* anywhere. It was precisely because historical films filled their frames with spectacle that superlative language seemed so fitting. In turn, the superlative nature of the films' attractions—tethered to grave historical narrative—required international recognition. *Veritas Vincit* was "the greatest German film. A work that will, like its famous predecessors 'Quo Vadis?,' 'Cleopatra' and others, garner the praise of the world."[43]

When working under the projected assumption of an international audience, historical films were always conceived and received in relation to other historical films. The films bore international ties through comparison and their incessant reaching beyond themselves. Because of this, "great" historical films began to create a sort of international archive of visual historical representation. This sentiment was reflected in the many lists of superior history films that included international titles. In this way, the history films were working together in a sense to create a standardized transnational lexicon of historical images.[44] The projections on and beyond the screen spirited the films' relevance and the viewers' understanding beyond theaters and national contexts into a shared corpus of popular historiography.

Lubitsch's films entered the international stage and realized the epic model by deploying spectacle in lavish detail while seamlessly integrating the same into entertaining narrative. Instead of subordinating all effects to a moral message in the tradition of Griffith, Lubitsch addressed international bodies through a distinct portrayal of detail and spectacle on the limits. Whereas the earlier Italian epics were known for massive set design (and destruction), camera movement, and unprecedented portrayals on screen, Lubitsch's historical films were primarily praised for his choreography of masses, historical realism, and streamlined narration. His trademark expertise was precisely the integration of these elements into the plot resulting in something like Tom Gunning's formulation of "tamed attractions."[45] This integration proffered a more "realistic" rendition of history that could allow for believable spectacle. An integral aspect of Lubitsch's keen deployment and taming of spectacle was his understanding of the shot frame, evidenced in his editing style.

Framing Historical Space

The utilization of the limit of the frame is well portrayed in Lubitsch's history films. In *Anne Boleyn*, the figure of Boleyn sits in a sailing ship and a medium close-up of her lavishly adorned upper body and face not only reveals her, but also conceals her in turn. The rocking motion of the ship is simulated through the rhythmic disappearance and reappearance of Boleyn into the frame. Not only does this entry of Boleyn act as a visual teaser, it also engages the container schemata of the audience. By bringing her medium close-up in and out of the frame through set-motion, the narrative is punctuated with an attraction of alternating absence and presence—reminiscent of early film's sense of temporality.[46] The attraction, however, is motivated in that it provides a historical reality effect, one that is produced by engaging the limits of the frame.

Passion's creation of space in the opening scenes also engages the container model in distinct ways. A near eyeline-match sequence, signaling offscreen glances, frames that film's protagonist, Jeanne's, position within the scene and reaches outward beyond the frame. Like the textual locating through the advertisement and title cards mentioned earlier, the audience is immediately confronted with the task of constructing the milliner's shop through visually referenced spatial relationships that extend beyond the visible shot. In such connective uses of space, Lubitsch frames his history with an intimacy that invites the viewer into the action. This is quite unlike Griffith's general eschewal of shot/reverse and POV shots.[47] Where Griffith sought objectivity in fictional stories, Lubitsch brought subjectivity and experience to historical figures through editing.

Lubitsch's proclivity for proper in/exclusion also revealed itself on the narrative level. As a French reviewer noted, Lubitsch's history of the French revolution "was true and respectful with very few liberties." He attributed this to Lubitsch's "simple trick[, which] was to only show a small part of the history and to leave the rest out."[48] It was true that even on a purely visual level Lubitsch was just as skilled at omitting from the frame as he was at filling it. The narrative magnitude, as well as small-scale editing, pushed out beyond the boundaries of the film frame by focusing grander visions in indexical microdisplays. This effect appealed to international audiences and critics and shaped a conception of historicity in the probability and pains-taking recreation of visual period detail and atmosphere. With a cinematic focus on visual display, history was becoming associated with spatializa-tion, texture, visibility, and motion that rendered in a new register "how it might have been."

Lubitsch's contemporaries were quick to praise his framing of spectacle, especially in period detail and the direction of masses. Attention to Lubitsch's spectacle also reveals the recurring project of visually connecting peoples and spaces by suturing viewers into seamless cinematic experiences. This is especially apparent in his handling of masses. Like Ramphis, the protago-nist of *Pharaoh*, as he joins and is lost in the streaming caravan of masses walking by, viewers and spectacles were similarly integrated into the flow of the story. Crosscutting shows Ramphis escaping the Ethiopian soldiers and then lying alone in a vast desert between shots of the flowing masses hailing from another direction. These two different locations, one with masses in motion and the other with a static single figure, converge when the caravan appears from behind the dune, upon which Ramphis rests. The protagonist is given water and then, in turn, takes the baggage of his rescuer and joins the stream of people. This give-and-take parallels the purpose of Lubitsch's interest in framing solitude against crowds.

The liminal and collapsing space between individuals and masses helped to visualize current preoccupations in historical disguise.[49] However, that is not to say the disguise had no historiographical effect. It put historical consciousness to work by allowing familiar and contemporary issues to be seen in other temporalities, among other peoples. Despite inevitable inaccu-racies, the masses have purpose in the hands of Lubitsch and allow for his-torical thinking through recognition and feeling. They are not merely scene architecture or geometrically bound into a unity, as is often the case with Fritz Lang's use of masses. Neither are they simply present as extras with no other purpose than to signify quantity, as Joe May might have directed them.[50] For Lang and May masses are contained in the frame, for Lubitsch they are individuals among and within masses who reveal the porous limits of each shot. The Lubitsch touch with masses "indexes the atomization of the individual as its dialectical pole."[51] The constant entering and exiting of masses in motion only accentuates this effect.

With masses, Lubitsch coupled his subjective filmmaking with offscreen/on-screen choreography. This brought a different dimension to historical filmmaking. A *New York Times* review of *the Loves of Pharaoh* stated, "no one is Herr Lubitsch's superior in the direction of masses."[52] This was because the experience of witnessing his direction had the "overwhelming" effect of "sweep[ing] the spectator out of the theatre ... and put[ting] him, without self-consciousness, before the reality of the titanic drama." As British film critic C. A. Lejeune noted, "no one before had so filled and drained his spaces with a wheeling mass, rushing in figures from every corner of the screen." This effect of masses against individuals and the use of the frame evoked a feeling of "multitude, and in contrast, loneliness."[53] It is no great surprise that diverse viewers seemed just as closely connected to the spectacles and the motion of masses, as the singular figures on screen.

Prosthetic Mobility

The exotic scenes and meticulous (re)constructions of history films offered a journey to another temporality, across imaginary boundaries. Beyond the insufficient label of pure escapism, the spectacle and detail in Lubitsch's work brought spectators out of previous limits and borders and spoke to a stifled *Wanderlust*. There existed a very real desire and necessity for escaping and traveling to other spaces. Especially since internalization and parochialism were the results of political isolation, Germany was seen to be at risk. After the war, the country had become like a province and was decidedly "begrenzt" (bordered/limited). In order to transcend this provinciality, "nothing was more pressing for Germans than to travel outside their borders." The hitch, however, was the inevitable result of the postwar economy: "who was still in a position to travel?"[54] In such an unfortunate economic situation, books and travel were unaffordable but some, like Dr. Edgar Beyfuss, hoped that movies could compensate and help to further society's intelligence and realm of experience.[55] As Arnold Zweig opined in 1922, the "Funktionslust" of film was found in vicariously "discovering a new land and desiring to have your own existence enlarged."[56] Coincidentally, the German version of *Around the World in 80 Days*, appearing in 1919, made this sentiment its premise. Of course, history and period films, along with exotic and travel films, offered chances to virtually visit other geographies and temporalities. History not only became something to be consumed but also experienced—escaped into. Cinematic history provided the primary means to go beyond the border virtually, when physical bodies could not.

The epic films themselves traveled beyond the borders of Germany precisely because of their virtuosic display. All three Lubitsch historical films were inducted into the international lists of exceptional photoplays and praised with superlatives. *Deception* only had to ride on the coattails of *Passion*'s reputation abroad. American reviewers noted its "promise[ ] to outrival the success scored by *Passion*."[57] And this was mostly realized. *Deception* screened to full attendance for an unparalleled four weeks at the

Rivoli Theatre. An ad in *Moving Picture World* proclaimed, "in all the years since the Rivoli opened, no picture has been held for more than two weeks! All box office records smashed; all records for length of run smashed." Such success was often the basis for justifying film's democratic and universal worth.[58] The third release upped the visual ante and as a spectacle, *Pharaoh* was praised as "the most complete motion picture ever made."[59] Just as significant as Lubitsch's ability to bring German production into the international arena of history making was his ability to show history by balancing spectacle and universally understood narration.

As a lavish spectacle, *Pharaoh* surely influenced Cecil B. DeMille's *Ten Commandments* a year later, yet Lubitsch included psychological depth. *The New York Times* reported, "in the midst of [*Pharaoh*'s] magnificent buildings, its Theban crowds and its battles of armies, a man's mind is revealed."[60] In reference to the cinematic regime of historicity, I suggest reading this review perversely. It is not just the pharaohs' mind that is psychologically revealed in the melodrama of the epic, but the mind of the international spectator who reacts to and understands historicity in spectacle. For international audiences, history on screen manufactured a mind that was cluttered with set pieces, monuments, stars, landscapes, distinct lighting, and only the very best take. But this was a "historic" experience.

The Politics of Historical Spectacle

The excessive monumentalism of historical films brought out two competing discourses concerning Germany's relationship to the rest of the world. This was in part due to the nature of film as at once international entertainment and a powerful weapon.[61] Both, imperial language—draping historical films' success abroad in terms of conquering and defeating, along with the mounting conception of history films as peace projects and international education were voiced. The now dominant historiographical narrative characterizing a downtrodden Germany seeking to regroup itself culturally through deep film investments was focused in the German reviews of *Passion*'s initial success. Sabine Hake is correct in stating that the "German newspapers and cultural journals often sounded like an imaginary continuation of the First World War, with film assuming the role of the avenging angel."[62] For instance, a German review of *Passion* engaged the battlefield of the film market by describing *Passion* as a means of conquering foreign powers. The projection of jingoism onto the film's success was evidenced in the form of the article. Artur Liebert framed an otherwise politically neutral synopsis of the film within his imperial language. The opening and closing statements lock the film into a context of the "battle against the impending foreign threat" by celebrating the film with the cry of "America, you are defeated!"[63]

In a "serious ballad of the Film importation" donning the cover page of *Film Kurier* in 1920, the author ends by counseling the reader not to worry because "German film is pretty good now too—and may the best [film industry] win!"[64] The review of *Dubarry* in Berlin praised Lubitsch's directorial genius as the best there is and that whether "friend or foe, whoever sees [Dubarry] must concede that."[65] Writers of *Lichtbild Bühne* realized how "splendid a weapon film could become in Germany's struggle for international recognition." The success of *Passion* evidenced the possibility of the once-defeated Germany to now "conquer the world market."[66] It is fair to say that before the ubiquity of Americanization in Germany from the mid-1920s on, the entrance into the film market was occasioned through historical film and was often framed in terms of imperial language, appearing to compensate for the losses of the war and colonies.[67]

There existed, however, an opposing view, an integrative notion of internationalism. Instead of merely continuing war in film or "ransacking the Allies' history," the films also created space for a discourse and sentiment of international relations and interconnectedness after the Great War. For this reason, it is important to consider more than just the initial rhetoric at home. Whereas a French reviewer saw *Passion* twice and, recognizing its potential, speculated about the political ramifications of successful German film abroad, the American company, First National, was much more accepting and marketed the film in the United States as having been filmed in "Northern Germany with an international cast."[68] A reviewer for *The New York Times* perpetuated the international flavor of the film and questioned whether an "apparently Teutonic Lubitsch," gained his "restraint, lightness of touch … [and] good taste" from working in Paris.[69] Hake highlights these ambiguities surrounding the film's national origins in early marketing to describe the international reception of *Passion* as one of "denial."[70] However, the film was also explicitly labeled "German-made" within weeks of its Philadelphia premiere in *The New York Times*, the newspaper with a much larger reading public than *MPW* or *Variety*.[71] Overwhelmingly, the initial questions of nationality surrounding the film resulted in its appraisal on its own terms. The consensus was largely in line with the American reviewer who called *Passion*, "one of the pre-eminent motion pictures of the present cinematographic age."[72] Additionally, despite the increasing presence of Germany on the world film market, the domestic colonial rhetoric surrounding *Passion* quickly dissipated.

The internationality of Lubitsch's work was occurring in content, style, and most importantly, reception, and this left his work open to nationalist criticism. Seen as nationalist projects, Pastrone changed the game with *Cabiria* and Griffith reset the stakes with *Birth of a Nation*, Lubitsch, however, stuck with historical events that had no intrinsic place in Germany's national archive. From revolutionary France, Tudor England, and ancient Egypt, his focus on "up for grabs" world history complicated nationalist uses of the past. In fact, aside from a handful of films, like the *Fridericus Rex* series and *The Nibelungen* adaptations, German history in general was only "very rarely" represented in German film after the war.[73] Of course, even the *Rex* series was carefully marketed to not "stink of propaganda" in order to ease foreign distribution.[74] Lubitsch's films deftly negotiated the creation of a universal language on film with internationally appealing historical display.

It was precisely because of the marketable cosmopolitan content that the author and scenarist Hanns Heinz Ewers' accused Lubitsch of "catering to foreign tastes." Ewers worried that foreign content with an absence of national myths would result in an "unhealthy mixture of racial and national characteristics that would eventually bring about the elimination of all differences."[75] Ewers' concern would be echoed in Stefan Zweig's 1925 essay, "The Monotonization of the World," after Americanization had swelled.[76] In response to Ewers, Lubitsch wrote, "the history of nations belongs to the world."[77] While the material belonged to the world, its presentation helped to shape one large "homogenous cosmopolitan audience."[78] Along with content aimed at bodily comprehension, the form made world history truly international and brought questions of national identity to the fore.

Putting the Nation in International

It was not merely foreign story material that was shaping Lubitsch's success. The internationality was occurring on a formal level. There is a marked adoption of foreign styles in Lubitsch's work. The American style, especially, seemed to increasingly suffuse his films. Yet Lubitsch was also inspired, as is evidenced in his critically acclaimed staging of masses, with classical painting (especially Velasquez) and the composition of extras found in Swedish films.[79] This mixture of influence led to a melting pot of cinematic presentation that generally aided his films' reception. By the time he made the eight-reel *Loves of Pharaoh*, its release in America reportedly required fewer title cards than most American five reelers.[80] The film's streamlined narration and photography exhibited a synergistic result of American and German editing. It is for such reasons that Kristin Thompson has defined Lubitsch as the "earliest ... to adopt the combination of techniques that constituted classical filmmaking," within Germany's delayed reception of Hollywood films.

The entanglement of American and German "styles" was tangibly evident in Lubitsch's "American-style facilities of the EFA studio" during his final years in Germany.[81] European Film Alliance (EFA) involved contractual agreements between Famous Players and Paul Davidson and although it was only a "marginal note in the history of film," the international alliance allowed for the creation of *Das Weib des Pharao* and the first world premiere of a German film on foreign soil.[82] The technology of artificial lighting, use of Bell & Howell all-metal cameras, and the transformation of glass house studios into dark studios were finally being implemented in Germany by 1922 and the EFA studios offered a glimpse into the future of German film-making.[83] The harnessing of light in the new dark studios helped make the films international. As Robert Florey explained in 1926, the manipulation of light in dark studios could make a film look "so normal that one would forget its nationality. Because of this, it becomes international. It can show on all the screens of the world, so that all audiences can understand it."[84] The merging of technology and national styles into an increased realism also shaped the presentation of history. The cinematic sense of the past was literally being illuminated and thereby internationalized.

What role did nationalism play in this slippery slope of international tastes? As much as foreign content and American film techniques informed Lubitsch's filmmaking, he saw himself and German film as providing a necessary alternative to the hegemonic carriers of the universal language most closely associated with Griffith.[85] Lubitsch felt that directors should aim to neither foreground their nationality nor suppress it, all while reaching world audiences. "'Supremacy on the world film market' is a catchphrase that neither represents nor grasps the situation as it really stands ... [a] film is good when the movie theaters in New York are just as sold out as those in Barcelona or Frankfurt. All filmmaking and all advancement of motion pictures must set out from this basic principle," stated Lubitsch. He was adamant that his films "succeeded because ... [he didn't] make German or American films, but rather Lubitsch films."[86] This conviction played out in his films, which quite literally connected viewing audiences in diverse locations.

The reflection of economic entanglement and film traffic was part of Lubitsch's stated conception of film. His view of nationalism and film-making contained the projected sentiment of international connection. As quoted earlier, Lubitsch maintained that a successful film meant it received "international applause and worldwide recognition" and that it was *under-stood* everywhere. His refusal to engage the equivalent of "debating whether Goethe or Shakespeare were the better writer" coincided with his belief that film transcended borders and brought nations together. This echoed other utopian thinkers, like the Weimar architect Erich Mendelsohn, who "advocated a kind of creative internationalism, a play of fantasy and aesthetics that might be based in national conditions but, in its working out, dissolves borders and brings people together."[87] The spatial framework of the nation was not about to disappear, but the notion of working outside, or on the limits of this framework was certainly evident in the production and consumption of visual history.

The flow of information on film, historical or otherwise, was saturated with hopes of national prestige and victory, as well as international pedagogy and social betterment. Of course, the film industries themselves stood to benefit from both sentiments. The formation of International Pictures of America, Inc., in 1922 was but another testament to the profitability and desire to connect nations and markets through film traffic. This entity was to "sell in the United States and Canada nothing but foreign-made pictures" and to "find an outlet abroad for films turned out [in the U.S.] by independent producers."[88] Several other corporations, following the model of EFA, popped up to capitalize on the forging film relations between countries. An advertisement for Ocean Films in *FilmKunst* in 1920 visually captured the state of affairs. The Ocean Films logo of a sailing reel of film is plastered on the head of a gigantic octopus. The octopus envelops the globe with its tentacles of film stock, stretching to the far reaches of the world. The visual result is a condition of both connection and control.

A clue to Germany's self perception in this tentacle-laden network of film can be seen in an article of *Lichtbild Bühne* in 1920, where the author took up the language of conquering. He opined that the German people needed to learn the model of self-marketing from the American film experts. That Germany was up against the "serious resistance" of a "dismissive attitude of the world" should only further motivate the German people to utilize film as an "advertising medium in the fight." The "fight" here, however, was not for political control but "for the recapturing of the German image," or reputation abroad.[89] This nuance provides an important insight into the deployment of militaristic language. The war, here, was for recognition and a place among the superpowers, who had recently written off Germany in the Versailles treaty.

As Franz Rode wrote in 1922, the world political landscape is a family of nations, wherein the more powerful can exploit the others. "It is the same in the world of film, where many members comprise a large family." In politics as in film, each member of the family functions like a limb of a body, each requires proper care and attention.[90] Each limb of the greater international body must learn to work together through consideration of the other. Germans recognized the necessity of carving out their own space as a member of the new world order. Even the much-contested Reich Motion Picture Law of May 12, 1920, functioned to ensure peaceful relations abroad. The law not only censored films that might have a "brutalizing or demoralizing effect" but also specifically those that would "endanger Germany's prestige or its relations with foreign countries."[91]

Utopia of Cinematic Historicity

The internationality of history films in content, style, and reception, while a threat in terms of economic inequality and the standardization of culture, bore a certain utopian potential. In Germany, Kurt Pinthus recognized the power of film as an expansion of human consciousness and experience. Especially since "every film is seen by 20 million people" there must be some unprecedented capacity for good, reasoned Pinthus. Film could transcend the very boundaries and limits hemming so many in after the war. Pinthus declared that often, films with great appeal would, "lead[] the individual across the entire surface of the earth, inserting him into varieties of life, from which he is otherwise excluded. And with the current international exchange of films between all countries, the possibilities for gaining knowledge of the world are becoming infinite."[92] This experiential element of historical film had, like film in general, an unparalleled effect. For the first time, history (as nonautobiographical scenes of the past) was becoming collective memories, and that across political borders.

Through cinematic representation "forgotten and murky events of history come back to life on film in a concise and universally comprehensible form. We suddenly find ourselves in distant lands; we see other peoples' customs and lifestyles, and the places where they live and how they work. People from every part of the earth file past us. And as knowledge of people expands, it seems to me, so does our love for people."[93] Pinthus' optimism for the medium highlights the imagined community of international audiences, who were eagerly led from their familiar lives into distant and unfamiliar horizons, even temporal ones, through embodied experience. This enriching capacity of silent film was presented by a modern technology that would, according to Pinthus' contemporary, Béla Balázs, return humans to premodern experience and communication.[94] Stripping away the accretion of languages, borders, and national frameworks, silent film could possibly bridge postwar nations by aiming at bodily comprehension.[95] The American counterpart to such utopian connections was the idea that movie houses were the new "Foreign Offices," which were much more effective and offered the "best means of producing greater world knowledge, world acquaintanceship, and hence, world peace."[96] Others more pragmatically formulated the idealistic and even mystical potential of film suggested by Pinthus and Balázs.

An important instance came at the banquet following the premiere of Fritz Lang's *Nibelungen* in 1924. Addressing the audience, Chancellor Gustav Stresemann "expressed the hope that the film would unite the German People and build a bridge to other nations."[97] Ultimately, this was the great potential of historical films, connection in difference. In this regard, the significance of historical film transcended nationalism, for as director Richard Oswald proclaimed, it was the genre of the history film itself that had conquered the "world market." It most closely resembled universal tastes and interest.

> In the framework of history, film found that Esperanto, which people throughout the entire world understand. The historical dress is the key to the international comprehension of human conflict. All of these conflicts have not fundamentally changed in the course of the centuries; they have only acquired a different rhythm, a different expression. They have bordered people off from one another nationally or according to various civilized circles. To bridge these differentiations and to only show humanity in a universally understandable form, is the deepest and most excellent mission of the historical film. Therein lies the secret of its worldwide validity, which no style can wrest from it.[98]

Stresemann's and Oswald's bridging of nations into a symbiotic web of interconnection was concretely occurring in the international contracts, trusts, and traffic of film.

Inevitably, some felt that Lubitsch's depictions were German propaganda to undermine national pasts. Yet even in the event of ransacking allied histories and presenting the warts of other national memories an unconvinced American reviewer challenged these supposedly victimized nations to "retaliate in kind." If they did then the "public at large may have the benefit of some interesting information not emphasized in the approved textbooks."[99] This was precisely what was at stake. Regardless of the divergent rhetoric accompanying the international historical films, they worked to make history experienced beyond textbooks. In other words, whether the interchange of historical film was accompanied by imperial or peaceful rhetoric the international sense and understanding of the past was being enlarged and homogenized as a common past.

History on film internationalized historicity and informed Griffith's grandiose plans as well as Lubitsch's attitude toward putting German history films on the map. In this revolutionary shift in the popular experience and conception of history, the power to (re)create the past was squarely in the hands of filmmakers and interconnected studios. Silent film was achieving what the League of Nations' political exclusivity was not. To this effect, an article in *Film-Kurier* in August of 1920 reported the integration of several national film industries. The international agreement to share films included America, Denmark, Sweden, and Germany, and both France and Italy had already expressed interest in joining. Such a "League-of-Nations-like-act of the film industry" was revolutionary in that the film industry could compensate for the political structure left by the Treaty of Versailles.

"Before the political League of Nations ... is realized, nations could be connected through this mighty deed of the film industry," stated the author. With several countries requesting induction into the "world trust," it was only a matter of time until "the rolling reel" of film would "embrace the whole globe and all nations."[100]

Notes

1 "Der Deutsche Spielfilm und das Ausland," *Der Kinematograph*, (1922) 780.
2 Griffith met with H. G. Wells. Not only had Wells recently published his popular history of the world, but that series also predated his future "*World Brain*" writings on making information available internationally for the betterment of mankind and the fostering of peace. Wells' *World Brain* in the 1930s was a revision of Wilhelm Ostwald's bibliographic conception from 1912. For these connections and more see Thomas Hapke, "Ostwald and the Bibliographic Movement," in *Wilhelm Ostwald at the Crossroads Between Chemistry, Philosophy and Media Culture*, ed. Britta Görs, et al. (Leipzig, Germany: Leipziger Universitätsverlag, 2005), 129–130. A similar but intensified project is currently underway with Google's world brain book scanning initiative.
3 *New York Times*, May 5, 1922, 34.
4 Kristin Thompson, *Herr Lubitsch Goes to Hollywood* (Amsterdam: Amsterdam University Press, 2005), 30.
5 Warren Buckland, *The Cognitive Semiotics of Film* (Cambridge: Cambridge University Press, 2000), 46.
6 Vivian Sobchack, "'Surge and Splendor': A Phenomenology of the Hollywood Historical Epic," *Representations* 29 (January 1, 1990): 28.
7 See Christian Metz, *The Imaginary Signifier: Psychoanalysis and the Cinema* (Bloomington: Indiana University Press, 1986), 14; Sabine Hake, *The Cinema's Third Machine: Writing on Film in Germany 1907–1933* (Lincoln: University of Nebraska Press, 1993), ix–xii.
8 Miriam Hansen, "Universal Language and Democratic Culture," in *Mythos und Aufklärung in der amerikanischen Literatur = Myth and enlightenment in American literature. Zu Ehren von Hans-Joachim Lang*, ed. Dieter Meindl and Friedrich W. Horlacher (Erlangen: Universitätsbund Erlangen-Nürnberg: Auslieferung, Universitätsbibliothek Erlangen-Nürnberg, 1985), 325.
9 Richard Maltby, "The Cinema and the League of Nations," in *"Film Europe" and "Film America": Cinema, Commerce and Cultural Exchange, 1920–1939* (Exeter: University of Exeter, 1999), 83.
10 Richard Nicolaus Coudenhove-Kalergi, *Pan-Europa*, 1.–5. (Wien: Pan-Europa-Verlag, [1923] 1982), 103.
11 Markus Krajewski, *Restlosigkeit: Weltprojekte um 1900* (Frankfurt am Main, Germany: Fischer Taschenbuch Verlag, 2006).
12 Ernst Troeltsch weighed these divergent attempts at relating world history in his review, "Eine Angelsächsische Ansicht der Weltgeschichte" *Historische Zeitschrift* 126, H.2 (1922): 271–79.
13 Siegfried Kawerau, *Synoptische Tabellen Für Den Geschichtlichen Arbeits-Unterricht Vom Ausgang Des Mittelalters Bis Zur Gegenwart* (Berlin: F. Schneider, 1921), iv.

14 Frederick William Roman, *The New Education in Europe* (London: Routledge and Sons, 1923), 196.

15 For the affliction and spread of such guilt, see Ernst Troeltsch's short essay of 1919, "The Dogma of Guilt," in *The Weimar Republic Sourcebook*, eds. Anton Kaes, Martin Jay, and Edward Dimendberg (Oakland: University of California Press, 1995), 12–15.

16 Freeman Tilden, "A World League of Women Can Prevent Wars," *The Ladies' Home Journal* (September 1922): 161.

17 Susannah Radstone and Bill Schwarz, *Memory: Histories, Theories, Debates* (Bronx: Fordham University Press, 2010), 334.

18 See Alison Landsberg, *Prosthetic Memory: The Transformation of American Remembrance in the Age of Mass Culture* (New York: Columbia University Press, 2004).

19 Miriam Hansen, "The Mass Production of the Senses: Classical Cinema as Vernacular Modernism," *Modernism/Modernity* 6.2 (1999): 68.

20 Siegfried Kracauer, *From Caligari to Hitler: A Psychological History of the German Film* (Princeton: Princeton University Press, 1947), 43–60.

21 Griffith also revisited *Intolerance* in 1922 by creating a "re-edit" from memory. See Miriam Hansen, *Babel and Babylon: Spectatorship in American Silent Film* (Cambridge: Harvard University Press, 1991), 133.

22 Scott Eyman, *Ernst Lubitsch: Laughter in Paradise* (New York: Simon & Schuster, 1993), 74.

23 "Philadelphia Society Attends Premiere of First National's Big Drama 'Passion,'" *Moving Picture World* 47 (December 4, 1920): 599.

24 David Pratt, "O Lubitsch, Where Wert Thou?" *Wide Angle* 13 (January 1991): 41–42.

25 Sabine Hake, *Passions and Deceptions: The Early Films of Ernst Lubitsch* (Princeton, NJ: Princeton University Press, 1992), 114.

26 Ernst Lubitsch, "Film Internationality," [1924], in *The Promise of Cinema: German Film Theory 1907–1933*, ed. Anton Kaes, Nicholas Baer, and Michael Cowan (Oakland: University of California Press, 2016), 298–300.

27 Robert Burgoyne, *The Epic Film* (New York: Taylor & Francis, 2011), 83.

28 Thomas J. Saunders, "How American Was It? Popular Culture From Weimar to Hitler," in *German Pop Culture: "How "American" Is It?*, ed. Agnes Mueller (Ann Arbor: University of Michigan Press, 2004), 58.

29 Anton Kaes, *Shell Shock Cinema: Weimar Culture and the Wounds of War* (Princeton: Princeton University Press, 2009), 134.

30 Andreas Wimmer and Nina Glick Schiller, "Methodological Nationalism and Beyond: Nation–State Building, Migration and the Social Sciences," *Global Networks* 2, no. 4 (2002): 302. For a detailed analysis of an individual silent film, see also Rick McCormick, "Ernst Lubitsch & the Transnational Twenties: The Student Prince in Old Heidelberg (USA 1927)," *TRANSIT* 10, no. 2 (2016), 1–10.

31 Julius Urgiss, "Der Internationale Geschmack," *Der Kinematograph* 806 (1922): 59.

32 Richard Schickel, *D. W. Griffith: An American Life* (New York: Limelight Edition, 1996), 457.

33 Burgoyne, *The Epic Film*, 2.

34 *Weltbühne*, December 21, 1922, 646.

58   *Entangling Histories*

35 Thomas J. Saunders, *Hollywood in Berlin: American Cinema and Weimar Germany* (Oakland: University of California Press, 1994), 58.
36 Thomas Elsässer and Michael Wedel, *A Second Life: German Cinema's First Decades* (Amsterdam: Amsterdam University Press, 1996), 69.
37 W. Stephen Bush, "Cabiria," *The Moving Picture World* 20 (May 23, 1914), 1090, quoted in *American Film Criticism, From the Beginnings to Citizen Kane* (New York: Liverlight, 1972), 80–82.
38 Kurt Pinthus, "Quo Vadis, Cinema? On the Opening of the Königspavilion-Theater," in *The Promise of Cinema*, Anton Kaes, Nicholas Baer, and Michael Cowan, eds. (Berkeley, CA: University of California Press, 2016), 186–89.
39 James S. McQuade, "Quo Vadis?" *The Moving Picture World* 16 (May 17, 1913), quoted in *American Film Criticism*, 64–66.
40 Gebhard Rusch, Helmut Schanze, and Gregor Schwering, *Theorien der neuen Medien: Kino, Radio, Fernsehen, Computer* (Paderborn, Germany: Wilhelm Fink Verlag, 2007), 220.
41 Quoted in Klaus Kreimeier, *The UFA Story: A History of Germany's Greatest Film Company, 1918–1945* (Oakland: University of California Press, 1999), 69.
42 Siegfried Kracauer, *Caligari to Hitler: A Psychological History of the German Film* (Princeton: Princeton University Press, 1947), 48.
43 Carl Boese, *Der Film* 15, April 12, 1919.
44 Anton Kaes, "History and Film: Public Memory in the Age of Digital Dissemination," in *Framing the Past: The Historiograpy of German Cinema and Television*, ed. Bruce Murray and Christopher J. Wickham (Carbondale: SIU Press, 1992), 315.
45 Wanda Strauven, *The Cinema of Attractions Reloaded* (Amsterdam: Amsterdam University Press, 2006), 52.
46 Tom Gunning, "Now You See It, Now You Don't," in *Silent Film*, ed. Richard Abel (New York: Continuum International Publishing Group, 1996), 76.
47 Don Fairservice, *Film Editing: History, Theory and Practice: Looking at the Invisible* (Oxford: Manchester University Press, 2002), 134.
48 Jacques Piétrini, La Cinématographie Française, Nr. 9/1920, quoted in "*Madame Dubarry—ein deutscher Sieg*," *Lichtbild-Bühne* 15 (April 10, 1920): 27.
49 Not only were returned soldiers and mobs of unemployed hired in the films but contemporary reviews compared the lines to the film with the masses on screen see "Philadelphia Society Attends," 599 and Thomas Elsaesser, *Weimar Cinema and After: Germany's Historical Imaginary* (New York: Routledge, 2000), 197.
50 Sabine Hake, "Lubitsch Period Films" in *Framing the Past: The Historiography of German Cinema and Television*, ed. Bruce Murray and Christopher J. Wickham (Carbondale: Southern Illinois University Press, 1992), 97 f.45.
51 Johannes von Moltke, *The Curious Humanist: Siegfried Kracauer in America* (Oakland: University of California Press, 2016), 127.
52 "The Screen," *The New York Times*, February 22, 1922, 22.
53 Caroline Alice Lejeune, *Cinema* (London: Alexander Maclehose, 1931), 64.
54 Joseph Friedfeld, "Jenseits der Grenze," *WeltBühne* 27 (July 6, 1922): 4.
55 E. (Edgar) Beyfuss and A. Kossowsky, *Das Kulturfilmbuch/Unter Mitwirkung Namhafter Fachleute Herausgegeben von E. Beyfuss Und A. Kossowsky* (Berlin: Carl P. Chryselius, 1924), 41.
56 Arnold Zweig, "Theoretische Grundlegung des Films in Thesen," *Das Tage-Buch* 10 (March 11, 1922): 372.
57 "Consensus of Published Reviews," *Moving Picture World*, May 7, 1921.

58 Hansen, "Universal Language and Democratic Culture," 327.
59 "The Screen," *The New York Times*, March 5, 1922, 80.
60 Ibid.
61 *"Madame Dubarry* in Amerika," *Lichtbild Bühne* 46 (13 November 1920): 20.
62 Hake, *Passions and Deceptions*, 120–21.
63 Artur Liebert, "'Madame Dubarry' der Aufschwung des deutschen Films," *Der Film* 38 (1919): 46.
64 Film-Kurier 77, April 15, 1920.
65 *Lichtbild Bühne* 38, August 9, 1919.
66 K. K., "Madame Dubarry–ein deutscher Sieg," *Lichtbild Bühne* 15 (April 10, 1920): 27.
67 Wolfgang Fuhrmann, *Imperial Projections: Screening the German Colonies.* New York: Berghahn, 2015, 267.
68 K. K., "Madame Dubarry–ein deutscher Sieg," *Lichtbild Bühne* 15 (April 10, 1920): 27. Eyman, *Ernst Lubitsch: Laughter in Paradise*, xxvii.
69 "Brought into Focus," *The New York Times*, January 30, 1921, X2.
70 Hake, *Passions and Deceptions*, 122.
71 *New York Times*, December 23, 1920, 15.
72 Eyman, *Ernst Lubitsch: Laughter in Paradise*, 74.
73 Oskar Kalbus, *Der Deutsche Lehrfilm* (Berlin: Carl Heymanns Verlag, 1922), 165.
74 In a letter from production manager Hans Neumann to assistant director Wilhelm Prager, exhibited in: "Der Falsche Fritz: Friederich II im Film" in Potsdam Filmmuseum, 2012.
75 Hake, *Passions and Deceptions*, 123.
76 Stefan Zweig noted how "Countries seem increasingly to have slipped simultaneously into each other." See Stefan Zweig, "Monotonization of the World," first published as "Die Monotonisierung der Welt," Berliner Börsen-Courier (Feb. 1, 1925). Weimar Republic Sourcebook is edited by Anton Kaes, Martin Jay, and Edward Dimendberg and reproduces the article in translation (University of California Press, 2016.)
77 Ernst Lubitsch, "Lubitsch Contra Ewers," *Lichtbild-Bühne* 52 (December 25, 1920): 29.
78 Siegfried Kracauer, *The Mass Ornament: Weimar Essays* (Cambridge: Harvard University Press, 1995), 325.
79 Eyman, *Ernst Lubitsch: Laughter in Paradise*, 79.
80 "Screen: Soundless Oratory" *The New York Times*, February 19, 1922, 71.
81 Thompson, *Herr Lubitsch Goes to Hollywood*, 109.
82 Klaus Kreimeier, *The UFA Story*, 74.
83 Thompson, *Herr Lubitsch Goes to Hollywood*, 111.
84 Robert Florey, "Deux ans dans les studios americains," quoted in Thompson, *Herr Lubitsch*, 109.
85 Ernst Lubitsch, "Brief," in *Lichtbild-Bühne*, December 25, 1920.
86 Ernst Lubitsch, "Film Internationality," [1924].
87 Eric Weitz, *Weimar Germany: Promise and Tragedy* (Princeton: Princeton University Press, 2009), 184.
88 *New York Times*, August 4, 1922, 21.
89 *Lichtbild Bühne* 43, 1920.
90 Franz Rudolf Rode, "Kino und Weltpolitik," *Der Kinematograph* 784 (February 26, 1922), front page.
91 Quoted in Kreimeier, *The UFA Story*, 65.

92 Kurt Pinthus, "The Ethical Potential of Film," in *The Promise of Cinema*, Anton Kaes, Martin Jay, and Edward Dimendberg, eds., (University of California Press, 2016) 388.

93 Ibid., 389.

94 D. Bathrick, "Der Unlgleichzeitige Modernist: Béla Balázs in Berlin," in *Filmkultur zur Zeit der Weimarer Republik*, ed. U. Jung and W. Schatzberg (München: K.G. Saur, 1992), 33.

95 Balázs' contentions have come to resonate with more recent cognitive studies into film, where visual expressions of emotions are shown to be near universals. See Joseph Anderson, *The Reality of Illusion: An Ecological Approach to Cognitive Film Theory* (Carbondale: Southern Illinois University Press, 1998), 133.

96 Walter Wrangler, "Films as Foreign Offices," *Daily Mail* (London) (December 10, 1921), 6, quoted in Desley Deacon, "'Films as Foreign Offices': Transnationalism at Paramount in the Twenties and Early Thirties" in *Connected Worlds: History in Transnational Perspective* (Canberra: Australian National University E Press, 2005), 140.

97 Kaes, *Shell Shock Cinema*, 135.

98 Richard Oswald, "Die Aussichten des Grossen Historischen Films auf dem Weltmarkt," *Der Kinematograph* 806, (1922): 60.

99 "Brought into Focus," *The New York Times*, April 24, 1921, X2.

100 "Eine Völkerbundtat der Filmindustrie," *Film-Kurier*, August 4, 1920, front page.

3   History Class at 16 fps

"Every student sees [film] with his eyes, feels it with his soul. Experiences it!"

—L. Kreiselmeier, 1925[1]

Through the connective tissue of historical films, in traveling reels and viewing experiences, history was truly becoming international and a force to be reckoned with. The shared wave of cinematic experience began to inform formal education. Throughout 1921, "hundreds of thousands" of Berlin school children visited the elaborately constructed set of Ernst Lubitsch's epic film, *The Loves of Pharaoh* (Figure 3.1). One can only imagine the students' delight walking through colossal models of historic space, reaching out and haptically experiencing ancient Egypt. Because the site was not "really" Egypt, nor traditional historiography, the teachers wanted the children to realize they were experiencing an exciting fictionalization. Although both textbook history and meticulous film sets were equally manmade mediations of the past the latter was more sensational and dangerous. This realization required action.

Upon returning to their classrooms the students received the assignment to tame the sensory field trip—the visual and monumental set designs—into analytical essays.[2] The excursion, at once worthy of educational use and necessitating written discourse, encapsulated the ambivalent attitude pedagogues harbored toward the film industry and its creations. The capacity for cinematic constructions (films and their accompanying sets, stars, and publicity) to shape society's relationship to the past demanded pedagogical intervention. Even when stoking historical consciousness, exciting bodily experience required restraint and semantic determination.

However, audiences of historical films, often figured as youth or children, were making their own sense of filmed history. Much of the effort to theorize the threat and potential of historical film for audiences grew from

Figure 3.1 Masses amid monuments in *Das Weib des Pharao*, 1921. Image
          courtesy of Stiftung Deutsche Kinemathek, Berlin.

the critics' mental construction of that very "audience." Weimar reform
pedagogues generally envisioned easily duped students, a situation which
required the instructor's verbal intercession. This view, in its pessimistic
understanding of reception, reflected the interwar sociological attitudes
toward the medium and foreshadowed critical theorists in the tradition of
Theodor Adorno, Max Horkheimer, and the Frankfurt School in general.[3]
Because of the (monolithic and theoretically imagined) audience's initial
ignorance of their subjugation (due to their false consciousness) they were
easily comparable to children.[4] Although teachers in the trenches of the
educational system interacted with youth directly, the authors of pedagogical tracts more often theorized improvement or, at most, extrapolated their
experience into abstract notions of formative education (*Bildung*). Then, as
an object of study, both pedagogy and critical theory required a constructed
group of passive recipients—immature and uncritical, these audiences were
essentially or literally children.

This conceptual framework was in line with pedagogical and psychological paradigms of the Weimar period, which saw children as generally

deficient. The professional objective was to find "ways of turning the immature, irrational, incompetent, asocial, and acultural child into a mature, rational, competent, social and autonomous adult."[5] Recent interventions in the growing field of the "history of childhood" have helped correct this narrow view, yet historically few thought otherwise. One of the few dissenting voices came from the iconoclastic Weimar theorist, Walter Benjamin.

Drawing on the singular ideas of Benjamin, this chapter argues for an alternative conception of audiences to historical films. Rather than requiring the "unnatural" thinking of historicist classroom instruction the audience's relationship to moving history on film can be better understood through Benjamin's conception of children as rebellious appropriators of information and objects placed before them. History films instructed viewers in the very construction of history. By effectively moving historical instruction from pure cognition to lived bodily experience, film catalyzed this revolutionary trend. The reception of cinematic constructions helped forge revolutionary connections between body and mind as they came to bear on historical representation. Although it would be unwise to completely divorce history from accuracy, focusing on reception and experience helps bring the force of historical film on historicity into relief. More intimate and personally meaningful, audiences' creative "miscognition" serves as a counter-portrayal of the result of film's historical instruction, against which pedagogues so diligently labored.

The potential for popular historical film to influence the Weimar classroom was apparent in initiatives like class trips to the ever-multiplying movie theaters. Echoing the Berlin trip to the Egyptian movie set, a field trip to a movie theater during the school year of 1922–1923, culminated in a written assignment on the topic, "How do I evaluate the film, *Fredericus Rex*?"[6] Such ambivalent applications of the medium were made both inside and outside the classroom. While some instructors tactfully incorporated images of the past and cinematic representation into classroom history lessons, others sought to reform movie theaters themselves into communal classrooms, by introducing more "educational" films, covering topics such as geography and history. However, efforts to integrate theaters and classrooms were attended by an entrenched sense of skepticism toward the medium. The term "historical film" seemed at times an oxymoron, an inevitably doomed coupling. Not only was popular film linked to the surface culture of Americanism and therefore shunned, but the ability of the medium to show a version of the past *in motion* also generated great concern. By exploring this ambivalence toward the potential of cinema in historical instruction, this chapter serves to, first, flesh out the history of film in the Weimar classroom, as well as theorize the medium's unique pedagogical possibilities across time for historical instruction.

Projecting Pedagogy

As a primary "means of intense worldwide information and suggestion" films after the Great War became a pedagogical and ethical concern.[7] For every nation this was due to photographic media's powerful portrayal and manipulative presentation of fact and fiction. The sentiment certainly informed the reception of historical films at home. Within Weimar Germany the tension between the use and abuse of history on film often hinged more on concerns of form and reception, rather than questions of historical fidelity. In practice, teachers regularly resorted to embedding filmic images of the past into written work or verbal lecturing, working against the open and direct work of monstration at the core of the filmic medium. At times, they even obscured the robust internationality of the history film genre by only introducing the few films directly treating German history to their student bodies.[8] This tendency to moderate the medium offered moments of deliberate engagement with the ethics of transmitting knowledge of the past and the formal influence of moving pictures on impressionable audiences.

Decisions on the proper use of historical film did not come easy. Even today, beginning "to think about history on film not simply in comparison with written history but in terms of its own is not an easy task."[9] The many opponents of the medium only exacerbated this difficulty. Often detractors have pointed to spurious content or fleeting images—a rapidity that offers "no time or space for reflection, verification, or debate."[10] In Theodor Adorno's words, film images "flash[] up … and slip[] away … [t]they are grasped, but not contemplated."[11] Although still uncertain of its place in the academy and classroom, several scholars have begun to speak of historical film as a distinct form deserving serious treatment. Along with this formal concession, Marnie Hughes-Warrington has distilled the current state of affairs into two additional areas of research: determining the specificity of the historical genre (apart from costume films, period films, nostalgia pieces, etc.) and the newly burgeoning line of inquiry involving "the expected or purported effect on viewers."[12]

This chapter is much less concerned with genre conventions and resolutely focused on the relationship between cinematic historical representation and the bodies of viewing audiences. This flattening of possible genre variety reflects the conviction that all filmic historical representation can shape a society's understanding of the past, historicity, and archive of experience. And whereas "we are only now beginning to appreciate" reception studies of historical film besides "what they represent on screen" the pedagogical anxiety of Weimar, coupled with the mounting legitimization of the medium, sparked insightful discussion in precisely this regard.[13]

By focusing on the medium and its effects on viewers, early debates had their own holes, false assumptions, and pseudoscientific methodologies, yet excavating them can help augment our current understanding. This type of historicization of popular historical consciousness continues the work of Vivian Sobchack, who has sought to "understand how historical consciousness emerges in a culture in which we are all completely immersed in images."[14] By turning to this earlier moment, when classrooms and theaters competed and converged, Weimar actually sheds light on moving images and their potential in historical instruction. It does this through the period's interest in media and its purported effect on the minds and bodily response of children. Whether corrupting or enlightening their historical understanding, one thing was certain: film got into viewers' bodies and affected them in powerful ways.

The movement of the images engendered concern in Germany regarding pedagogy, ethics, and the specific role of the historical film genre. It was the hurried sixteen frames per second flashing before the students' eyes that provided the most anxiety as well as promise. Indeed, moving pictures proved to be a boon in speeding up history lessons, engaging students, and directly showing proposals of how the past looked. Working off a developing urban culture of visuality, film spoke powerfully to youth and adults alike, providing history beyond dry dates, trends, and charts. Because of this promise and the uphill battle teachers already fought against the expanding film industry for their students' attention, it became necessary to assess the potential of the medium.

Theoretical engagement with the medium of film and its instructional potential, although not unprecedented, was still novel. In Wilhelmine Germany several articles had appeared, weighing the potential of cinema for historical understanding.[15] However, following the devastation of the Great War, borders, methods, expectations, and the course of history itself seemed broken up, all of which required reconsideration. The resulting reflections on the intersection of film and historical instruction brought the anxieties and hopes of the medium into relief for another important reason. As in other lands, but perhaps even more pronounced in Germany, the concern flared up in relation to the youth of the nation and deeply ingrained notions of culture. And Germany's intellectual history of privileging depth over surface heightened the stakes of history on film.[16] This was a cultural concern. Reevaluations of school instruction and youth attendance at movie theaters converged in the discourses surrounding postwar history films.

In the debates on cinema and history, teachers inhabited a prominent position, especially since "their position of cultural authority represented one of the few forces which could counter the most damning attacks on the film industry—its harm to children."[17] It was the political clout of the pedagogues and their sympathizers that enabled the overhaul of historical instruction in early Weimar. They were among those who "made it possible to inaugurate a complete change in both the subject-matter and the spirit of the history-teaching."[18] Both of these developments, in updating history teaching and experimenting with film use in the classroom, began to dovetail.

As was evidenced in instruction manuals and the selection of essay topics, the new school of history instruction made the past digestible and scientific at the same time. The sociological inflection of the new school of history included detailed anecdotes, comparative data, and multiple media source material. As Barbara Hanke relates, the essay themes in school "aimed at emphasizing the cultural side of historical happenings" by turning away from monarchical-dynasty relations and toward "treatment of sources or historical cultural media."[19] Essay topics included: "the Bismarck monument in Hamburg" and "Images of German Revolution of 1848 according to source reports." And directly reflecting the popularity of the *Fridericus Rex* historical film series another essay theme read "why has the figure of Frederick the Great become so popular?"[20] The newer history enlarged the capacity to legitimize and earnestly engage the popular level of the historical culture.

In accordance with the call for new history after the Great War, "[o]rders were given that the history-texts should be re-written in the new spirit" and a concrete example of this was the appearance and wide adoption of *Synoptische Tabellen für den geschichtlichen Arbeits-Unterricht* led by Siegfried Kawerau.[21] The textbook captured the spirit of the new history by revealing the sociological inflection of the past presented in an open format, allowing the instructor the freedom of personal style. The textbook explicitly stated its intentions against the memorization of information and instead positioned itself to bolster the instruction of students in the "method of getting along with source material" itself.[22] Stripped of all the narrative expansion, the *Tabellen* resembled a bare film scenario awaiting embodied clarification. The new format could function outside the strict linearity of traditional historical instruction. The instructors were to read through the text "not completely in a successive or simultaneous fashion," but to flesh out the skeletal presentation of historical tidbits with their own performative interpretation in the classroom. This new format, open and bare, was the "first step in helping history teachers" present history as "the form and fate of the human race," rather than mere "external events."[23]

Although the book's main author, Kawerau, was at times a bit of an outsider to the otherwise conservative discussions on historical instruction he did not go unheard.[24] The efforts of Kawerau and others to reform history instruction garnered the praise, "here history becomes science, which means: the simultaneous exploration of truth and the personal life of the individual, where each [student of history] comes to feel his part in the development of mankind." These were positive developments since former history instruction had been too caught up with sensational hero-worship and generally "avoided the true face of raw reality." By "showcasing developments and placing the individual within the larger laws of development," history was taking on a sociological hue.[25] History also increasingly took on the descriptors of film, which could represent raw, bare reality by capturing and recording surface.

Kawerau was convinced that the innovative new history would shape politically and socially informed citizens. The end goal of all the pedagogical shuffling was a projected ideal student of history that would enjoy a new and deeper felt relationship to the past. Students were supposed to "learn to self-sufficiently develop historical contexts and to recognize the thorny nature of their compilation and interpretation."[26] What role film would play in the formation of new history and the development of historical acumen in the student body was still to be determined.

Lights, Camera, Reflection

The topical concerns of historical instruction were discussed in the periodical *Vergangenheit und Gegenwart*. As the primary organ for history teachers in the immediate postwar years the publication concerned itself chiefly with questions of "content selection, the relationship to social studies, and essays on the meaning, merit, and objective of historical instruction in schools."[27] Gustav Würtenberg's contribution to the periodical in 1928 contemplated the relationship between the history class and cinema. Even if a bit late to jump on the media-advocacy bandwagon, the article was quite progressive, considering the largely conservative tone of the periodical. In the brief article, Würtenberg claimed that students lacked interest in the past and that teachers needed to teach "with details and anecdotes and make it an experience oriented toward the present."[28] Film could help make the past present *as an experience.*

For Würtenberg, history was only meaningful in the emotional connection individuals have to it, or in the "enthusiasm it evokes." Emotional enthusiasm should also foster greater pedagogical hopes. Not only should students develop "historical thinking" but also the "desire to participate" as a fellow citizen in society."[29] For this reason and in view of the potential of historical film, Würtenberg called for a shift in orientation: away from content to the students themselves.[30] In the effort to make history into an "experience" geared toward the present, film afforded new possibilities.

The increased concern for a new type of historical instruction could not be separated from the increased presence of visual history. A singular example of this was the *Reichsschulkonferenz* of 1920 where the film department of the chancellery actually explored the potential of film in instruction.[31] During this same time, several reform groups established periodicals such as *Bild Archiv* and *Bild und Schule*, both of which provided concrete and theoretical defenses for the implementation of film and images in classroom instruction. These reform pedagogues explicitly meant to put the "Bild" back into *Bildung* through fostering engagement with the new medium.[32] All of these developments helped to validate the medium as historiographic in some regard and superbly instructional in general.

While the images could be vibrant and engaging, such publications often urged teachers to provide proper accompanying instruction in the classroom in order to mitigate the power of photographic media. This threatening power was, as German cultural critic Siegfried Kracauer articulated it, a capacity to blow over the past and conceal distinguishing characteristics, as if "under a layer of snow."[33] From the vantage point of the lectern the flashing images required verbal taming and supplementation to make them manageable and appropriately historical. It was common counsel to suggest that the use of "motion pictures must develop organically from the lecture. It must conduct itself according to the lecture, like the dot of an 'i' or the end of a sentence in relation to its beginning. It must be the logical consequence of the lecture."[34] As the figurative language here aptly enacts, the filmic images were to be wrapped in the clothing of discourse and traditional orthography. Visual, icon-heavy motion pictures were transformed into the "dot of an 'i'" or a "period at the end of a sentence"—literally translated into secondary elements of writing. The *Lichtspiel* had to be integrated into the *Lehrplan* and should be accompanied by still images and lecturing.[35] In this mode the provocative and mnemonic images could be taken on institutionally through methodological compromise. However, the interaction was always, like the field trip to the "ancient Egyptian" film set, a translation of visual data into written and verbal discourse in order to insure intellectual depth.

The perceived necessity of supplementary words was also taken up in a contemporary reflection on film by Austrian author Hugo von Hofmannsthal. In his "Substitute for Dreams," Hofmannsthal includes a biting depiction of masses drawn toward images and away from language, which paralleled the difficulty in bridging the divide between popular/commercially successful history films and purely instructional history. This was just another manifestation of the pedagogical concern that there existed an "ever growing gulf between education [Bildung] and entertainment [Unterhaltung]."[36] Although films could be deliberately manufactured to convey educational information as their primary purpose they lacked popular draw. As with traditional written history, in Hoffmanthal's estimation the lecture halls bear the written designation "'Knowledge is Power,' but the cinema, calls more strongly: it calls with images."[37]

Theaters could, however, use images to educational ends. Since the audience that actually knew and consumed educational films was a "pathetic amount" in comparison to "the hundred thousand people who go to the movies daily" it was advisable to package the instructional film as part of the sideshow. In order to pull this off the educational features would also have to be short and interesting.[38] In Wilhelmine Germany the establishment of "wanderkinos" and "scientific" cinemas had attempted this feat of instructing the nation while utilizing the locales of the most modern form of leisure with varying success.[39] The difficulty in marrying the popular and sensational form with intellectual engagement and uplift was never straightforward.

Even with educational films an accompanying lecturer was preferred, since the moving images alone were too open ended.[40] Not only were images ambiguous and open to varied imaginative reactions and interpretations, but films inevitably lied and this presented an enormous difficulty for a society entrenched in the nineteenth century historicist relationship to the past. Film's ontological realism necessarily required the details of filling the screen with speculation, ideas, and visual harmony—precisely the historical materialism a historiographer could omit from writing. In order to film a historical scene, directors, set designers, costumers, and a slew of other workers had to place furniture, people, architecture, lighting, and choreography in the frame. All this sensational detail could never fulfill the requirements of historicism in the cold exactitude of science. Historical film was, from the outset, damned both ways: not accurate enough, while being much too literally accurate. This attribute of filmed history then played a role in initiating the longstanding debates on accuracy and license.

Content of the Form

In 1925, Oxford Professor S. E. Morison called for a more thorough teaching of American history in schools in order to "offset the distorted view of American life presented" by American motion pictures. In his estimation the youth were "getting their ideas" about American history from these Hollywood films, which were "produced for an American market and prove a romantic compensation for humdrum life on Main Street." The "inaccurate" portrayals of the past were being spread across the globe affecting more than domestic audiences.[41]

Beyond their dangerous internationalism, history films were, for others, inevitably unfit for instruction. German Professor Konrad Lange argued this was because "an artificial self-placement in any long gone or other-wise unfamiliar milieu must always lead to falsification and archeological theatrical polish." Lange's logic meant directors should only represent what they themselves have witnessed or experienced. Because of the penchant for artistic license, historical films were impeded by the same problems inher-ent in historical painting.[42] Of course, this impulse to denounce inaccuracy in historical representation continues today and as a sort of "game" has become a fixture in the marketing and reception of historical films.[43] But the game of ripping a historical film apart based on historical fidelity (to current historiographical interpretations) often elides the medium-specific qualities of history films.

Unfortunately, the longstanding focus on inaccuracy and the pitfalls of history on film has led to stagnating redundancy in writing about his-tory films. Many historians through the turn of the twenty-first century have maintained the legacy of anxiety "about 'accuracy,' 'authenticity,' and 'respect for the historical record.'"[44] But the cultural significance of his-torical film will not be sufficiently clarified through writing solely about content. The assumption that history films transmit data that is true or false obfuscates cinema's role in shaping and responding to shifts in historical thought and experience. Although historical accuracy and research were integral to many films, the deeper issue lays in the medium itself and its effect on embodied audiences.

These concerns were already recognized in early Weimar and, along with the medium of film shaping a widespread "sense of the past," visual culture across a broad spectrum was seen to be proliferating. This fresh visuality served to refine thought about media and its implementation. The cultural orientation toward image over written language reflected a general societal shift from symbols to indices and icons.[45] Already in 1916, the psycholo-gist Hugo Münsterberg remarked that history in the "last two decades was deeply influenced by the columns of the illustrated magazines. Those men who reached millions by such articles cannot overlook the fact—they may approve or condemn it—that the masses of today prefer to be taught by pictures rather than by words."[46] Many feared the effects on historical under-standing and society in general if cinema continued to eclipse written dis-course. Indeed, the photographic medium's relationship to history was an ethical one.

Visuals alone, especially those of motion pictures were too surface— too fleeting for intellectual depth or understanding. This was the concern voiced in 1919 by outspoken conservative journalist Wilhelm Stapel in his article titled, "Homo Cinematicus," which appeared in the widely read pages of *Deutsches Volkstum*. Stapel was convinced that children, who reg-ularly attended the movies "suffer[ed] psychic damage form the *form* of the presentation alone." This novel insight, despite its spurious conclusion, grounded the anxiety in medium specificity. The turn away from scandalous content and toward the medium itself radicalized earlier efforts to expose the dangers of film. Stapel went beyond Albert Hellwig's 1910 study of the detrimental effects of cinema on children, where "sleeplessness, bad dreams, the destruction of good taste, the encouragement of criminality and sexual problems" were all attributed to content and specific "Schundfilme," or trashy films.[47] Although some earlier writers had denounced the biological effect of the flickering image on the eye, they hadn't extended this condition of projection to intellectual regression.[48] Stapel's damnation of form spoke to a growing tendency to take film seriously and on its own terms. The form of cinema alone destroyed principled integrity. Stapel further argued, "the sheer fact that the viewer becomes habituated to the flashing, fluttering, and twitching images of the flickering screen slowly but surely destroys his psychic and, ultimately, his moral stability."[49] A nation with increasing numbers flooding the cinemas was in danger of losing its depth of *Kultur* and moral steadiness.

The cinema—whether it was showing history, sex, crime, or adapted classics of literature—was "*constructing a new human type, inferior in both its intellectual and moral capacities; the homo cinematicus.*" This fear surrounding the ethical consequences of new media was characteristically focused on the younger demographic, on those who might be most vulnerable to its pernicious effects. After literature in the nineteenth century, film was also subjected to this circular argumentation in the early twentieth, as were television and comic books decades later. Stapel's style of alarmism resurfaced in a highly publicized hearing following the publication of *Seduction of the Innocent* (1954), when German émigré Fredric Wertham stood before the US congress and denounced the vile influence comic books and popular media were exercising over young men. But unlike Stapel, Wertham's psychological studies, and many such denouncements, were rooted in content and advertisements. The concerns about film in Weimar Germany foregrounded the medium itself and formal considerations of influence. Film could potentially change the psychological and, therefore, intellectual makeup of audiences. The images were affecting bodies.

Stapel's fears concerning the effect of a medium on cognition are more closely echoed today in discourses on the Internet. In his widely read article, "Is Google making us stupid?" Nicholas Carr popularly renewed this fear in the face of new media by describing how "the Net seems to be … chipping away [his] capacity for concentration and contemplation. [His] mind now expects to take in information the way the Net distributes it: in a swiftly moving stream of particles. Once [he] was a scuba diver in the sea of words.

Now [he] zip[s] along the surface like a guy on a Jet Ski."[50] While Carr explicitly piggybacks Marshall Mcluhan in his connections between media and thought, Stapel offers his alarmism some forty years prior to Mcluhan's *Understanding Media*.[51] Stapel's worries, however, include the top down influence of a medium on an otherwise passive and victimized audience. The interactivity and volitional jumping from hyperlink to hyperlink of Carr's new media concerns are nowhere to be found in Stapel's monolithic youth audiences. Despite these important distinctions, the focus on medium in both contexts can be seen as reactionary. Yet, in their own novel and alarmist ways, these media theories at least endow the forms with cultural formative power, rather than quibbling over accuracy or content.

Space and Time

Contrary to Stapel's anxiety, others saw a profound potential in the medium, specifically for shaping youth and enhancing instruction. In a German review after the American release of Lubitsch's film *Passion*, the author remarked, "the sets and details are illustrious and impressive. 'Passion' has great dramatic, historical, and instructional merit."[52] Just what was the "merit" of history films in historical instruction? This question was taken up in a short-lived debate between Paul Eller and Gustav Benkwitz in the pages of *Der Kinematograph* in 1921. Moving beyond the repetition of declarations that film makes "instructional material come alive"[53] or provides such in an "unforgettable form,"[54] Eller and Benkwitz teased out the very properties of historical film through their disagreement. A central point of contention, around which this "Geschichtsfilmdebatte" revolved was the roles of space and time in historical instruction and understanding. This core issue effectively joined media theories with ethically charged pedagogical concerns. They also helped clarify how visual perception in historical instruction could be cinematically tied to lived embodied experience.

Paul Eller set the terms of the discussion by recognizing that the traditional process of historical instruction in the classroom involved "successively considering the individual pages of history and then synthesiz[ing] them into a totality with the help of imagination and memory."[55] It was no mistake that Eller singled out history occurring on "pages," since the traditional form of historical instruction was limited to this sequential deployment of information in time and to a dated medium. This method forced the student to synthesize and compile the many and diverse details. For Eller, the ability of film to render both a spatial and a temporal continuum illustrated its superiority in providing a fuller experience of history. Eller's use of the terms *nacheinander* (one after another, or in a time sequence) and *nebeneinander* (simultaneously present in space) served to mine a tradition of treating the specificity of visual arts as well as the phenomenological experience of the world.

Harking back to Gottfried Lessing's contemplation on the Laocoon Group statue as a means to delineate media distinctions, Eller used the terminology to equally describe the potential of cinema. Already in Lessing's seminal work a contrast is made between the attributes of poetry and the plastic arts.[56] Here the guiding characteristic of poetry is that it must occur in time, or provide the images, narrative, and details in the course of a sequence (nacheinander). The plastic arts, however, provide a spatial display (nebeneinander). Because of this distinction Lessing felt that statuary and painting should focus on the most pregnant moment to depict and that is was only capable of gesturing toward motion by hinting at the next or preceding moment. This partitioning of the arts via a spatial and temporal continuum reflected a focus on the reception of the artwork.[57] For Lessing the sequence of poetry allowed for more tolerance of mistakes or low points, whereas the plastic arts were to be appreciated in their present stillness and a focus on bodies.

However, with film Lessing's statues come to life and move through time and space. The added motion nuances Lessing's estimation of visual art. The conceptual shift is rendered visually in Paul Leni's 1924 film *Waxworks*, when several wax figures are brought to life through constructing stories within the story. The narrative potential of visualizing the effigy in motion is exploited and the writing of their tales is made cinematic for the audience. With this technological development a more topical comparison of media became that of writing and film. Of course, authors of the period did experiment with filmic conventions in literature and perhaps most widely praised, James Joyce engaged the limits of his medium, with *Ulysses*.[58]

Along with other "big city novels," such as *Berlin Alexanderplatz* and *Manhattan Transfer*, which used modernist narrative techniques including "movie-like images," *Ulysses* thematized media itself.[59] Not only does *Ulysses* appropriate filmic components, it explicitly states the nacheinander and nebeneinander of its own narration through Stephen Dedalus's thoughts by quoting Lessing.[60] "I am, a stride at a time. A very short space of time through very short times of space. Five, six: the *nacheinander*. Exactly! And that is the ineluctable modality of the audible. Open your eyes! If I fell over a cliff that beetles o'er his base, fell through the nebeneinander ineluctably."[61] Traditional historical instruction without film followed suit with Dedalus by closing its eyes and only taking in the nacheinander of successive information. By restoring sight and allowing both sequence and spatiality, film brought something distinctive to the teaching of history. Lessing's terms of succession and simultaneity proved equally fruitful for Eller's thinking and defense of the medium.

The terms also indicated that history on film, then, presented pasts within viewpoints that largely coincided with viewers' biological vision. These lenses to a staged past follow human existence in the convergence of both a temporal and a spatial continuum. History on film was history for embodied subjects. It was from Immanuel Kant that Kuno Fischer related the knowledge: "from the myriad things, which we perceive through the senses, we abstract their common traits and create out of this their totality: or conceptual type. In just this way, time and space are drawn from their perception, abstracted from sensual impressions." In other words, "we perceive things as they are apart from or next to each other, as they are either simultaneously there or as they successively follow."[62] Again, this was the conceptual tradition Eller was drawing from to illuminate the potential of the past represented on film.

Although it was ambiguous whether Kant understood space and time as subjective or objective phenomena, it was clear that the human experience of the world was to be found in this relationship to the surrounding environment. Since "Kant thought that space was the form of our outer experience, and time the form of inner experience," the categories suffused the attempt to grasp the lived world.[63] These two aspects in play brought the teaching of history closer to real life. This was precisely what many history teachers sought—a means of modernizing history and making it connected to daily life. This formal connection to the phenomenological experience of the world would not only make the past more meaningful, but update the experience of thinking about other temporalities. By hinting at the phenomenological experience of history films for children in classrooms, Eller initiated a thought experiment that would be subsequently fleshed-out by the late writings of Maurice Merlau-Ponty on childhood.[64] But the general idea was also pursued in Walter Benjamin's writings and radio lectures about children, to which we will return. The spatial and temporal structures of experience underlying each of these theorist's descriptions of child pedagogy were central to Eller's advocacy of history on film.

Eller's remarks inspired Gustav Benkwitz to reply with an opposing view. Benkwitz was convinced that history on film could only be historical source material for later periods. "Film is a document, the best possible document of life, that is to say a witness of all things contemporary. And in this way it is truth and a historical source for those who come after us." Benkwitz saw all filming as a document of its profilmic events for future audiences.[65] He would only budge enough to allow that it was by all means possible "to record circumstances, practices, customs, which extend from ancient times into our day." This might include filming ancient ruins or existing vestiges of earlier periods as they endure today, but only because they are already naturally part of the visual present. As others noted, the accretion of such archival footage could lead to increasingly well-documented historical instruction.[66]

Robert Flaherty's success with *Nanook of the North* (1922) and *Moana* (1926) realized Benkwitz's contention by staging/recording timeless cultures seemingly untouched by modernity. The documentary drive for film was also evidenced in the International Iconographical Commission's description of films meriting archival preservation. These were films, "which record a person or period from the time after the invention of cinematography and without dramaturgical or 'artistic' purposes those films which present a visual record of a definite event, person or locality, and which presuppose a clearly recognizable historical interest inherent in the subject matter."[67] This impulse was another symptom of the filmic relationship to the past—a sense of time and historicity that merited photographic ties to *making* history through recording.

However, "to want to record circumstances that existed before film" was for Benkwitz, as for Professor Lange, absolute "nonsense." Such an endeavor "would be, on scientific grounds, deception."[68] For Benkwitz staging history on film exploited the ontological realism of the camera by reproducing the manufactured profilmic as history and such a process was unhistoriographical. Because of this situation there was, for Benkwitz, no cinematic history "before" the photographic medium. There was no filmic access to events and figures predating the medium of film and the mere desire to undertake such a feat would inevitably result in fraud. Benkwitz effectively flattened Eller's media-specific advocacy for staged history on film into a merely content-producing medium.

Eller seemed surprised with Benkwitz's response. He wrote a follow up article stating that Benkwitz was unable to see the difference between film as instructional (as a synthesized version of the past) and film as a document of a past (as a source), but for Eller the contrast had to be made. The history film cannot—and should not—show true life as it simply already exists before it, this would be source recording rather than history telling. For Eller these were two different types of film, generically the difference between actualities and history films. And if Benkwitz wanted to call history films a "Schwindel" then Eller felt Benkwitz needed to apply it to the "oral instruction without film as well, which also provides no real life and is much more cumbersome and less effective than lecture with film. Class should have both the lecture and the images."[69] The distinction was important because it would foster critical understanding of the medium that would enhance future use.

However, the ability of film to be edited, sequenced, and manipulated allows just this type of historiophoty, as Hayden White has coined it, to occur.[70] The sequencing and capturing of any construction put before the camera are what makes Eller's filmed history so promising. The sum of Eller and Benkwitz's arguments actually turns the tables on the denunciations made by Lange, Morison, and Stapel. Because history films immediately become a staged past and a document to their moment of production and exhibition both conceptions merge. Especially since feature films are comprised of "shots that are traces of a past real incorporated into an overall sequencing process,"[71] the possibility of writing history in light comes from the capacity of reconstructions, reenactments, and edits to construct the past for a viewing present. By this definition even a perfect document(ation) would never be "history" until it is edited into a sequence.[72] In other words, it is edited narrative film that might most effectively do history and be history, which arguably also allows for more appeal and identification for audiences.

In fact, the positions taken by Benkwitz and Eller could be correlated with those of Marc Ferro and Jean Luc Godard against Pierre Sorlin and Christian Metz.[73] All films are fictions, yet every film is in some way a document. As Fritz Lang recognized in 1924, "A future time will have it easier ... to make our chaotic time period come to life. The future will open a canister of condensed life, by playing a film. This is a piece of history from that time."[74] With the revisitation of the ever-expanding lexicon of historical representation on film, these possibilities join forces. For instance, as we now watch Lubitsch's history films in archives or in restored digitized form they are certainly both document to an early Weimar past and remain also proposals of their own narrative staged pasts. It is for this very reason that history films made to be as popular as possible (striking a cultural chord as widely as possible) grow to enlarge both a represented past and a consuming past present. In fact, for pedagogical purposes, it worthwhile to select dated history films if the desire is distancing the audience from the film through the creation of a critical gap.[75] This move can often work against the invisible draw of the film and (re)construct a temporal frame for the audience to deal with history film's double exposure in a pedagogical setting and historicist mode. However, there is more going on for children and childlike audiences of history films. Critical and historicist explication of the past is not necessarily the medium's primary power.

Thinking in Images

Eller's optimism for the medium, in transforming historical instruction, echoed Griffith's earlier pronouncement that "six moving pictures would give these students more knowledge of history of the world than they have obtained from their entire study."[76] Similarly, in Johannes Molzahn's 1928 article, "Stop Reading! Look!" he projected the future of education in the deft use of images. The turn to instruction with images not only reflected the tempo of the time with abrupt changes but also the management of time and efficiency.[77] Working against the mechanization of the intellect, Molzahn's view partook of the very discourse of Taylorist efficiency and instrumentalization. Efficiency was a cherished trait in Germany and even outsiders saw the country as the most efficient and industrial in youth instruction.[78] Images in motion meant efficient learning. The rapidity of displaying sixteen frames per second was seen to mirror film projection's physiological and technological capacity to offer more, through gaps and the persistence of the retina's construction of an after-image. While providing quicker and flashier history, it "tricked" the eyes and historical understanding. Films could more efficiently fulfill the role of the historian by "conjuring" up "not only a plastic image of the past but also one full of life."[79] For many, there remained a fine line between flickering time conservation and superficial instruction.

As an attempt at testing the effects of history in motion for students, Prussian schools established projectors and instructional films throughout the district in 1920, with the intent of reporting their results the following year.[80] While select areas of Germany flirted with the new medium, the Yale Chronicles of History project in the United States put the effort into full force. Yale University oversaw the transfer of *The Chronicles of America* into a film series. In many ways, this project pursued Griffith's earlier desires of world history on film,[81] albeit with more scholarly clout and merely a national focus and pool of contributors.[82] The experiment was gaining attention abroad as well.

Yet, the whole endeavor bore the stamp of institutional approval from the academy. Yale University made Rex Ingram, the director of *Four Horsemen of the Apocalypse*, an honorary PhD and asked him to helm the *Chronicle* series.[83] These forty- to forty-five-minute films, supervised and fact-checked by academic historians, were the American response to film as historical instruction. "Not one foot of film will be released until it has had the official sanction of Professors Farrand and Spaulding, who will be assisted in an advisory capacity by eminent authorities representing public school as well as university opinion." This arduous work also included "research of the most exacting kind."[84] And with the *Chronicle's* photoplays, cinema was said to have "arrived at historical authenticity."[85]

As commercial products the films flopped. The overwhelming sense was that the "series was a worthy idea stifled by academic pedantry." The project had gone too far in the direction of historicism, wasting precious time and money on seemingly insignificant details.[86] Nevertheless, the *Yale Chronicles* effort allowed for analysis of the results of wholesale incorporation of film in historical instruction.

In 1928, Daniel C. Knowlton and J. Warren Tilton conducted extensive studies in classroom history instruction with the use of the *Chronicles* series. The research was done at Troup Junior High School in New Haven, Connecticut in seventh grade classes. Their varied tests and analyses drove them to reach the conclusion that the filmed histories caused students to read more supplementary history for longer periods of time in class.[87] Although the comparisons were made between "good oral instruction on the one hand, and on the other, the same amount of instruction, five-sixths oral and one-sixth visual," the critical difference was the small fraction of motion pictures in the classroom. Not only did students read more, but the "photoplays contributed materially to the gaining and retention of worthwhile knowledge, particularly knowledge of interrelationships, other than time" and "produced more pupil participation in classroom discussion."[88] Despite some glimmers of hope, researchers lamented the student's film-induced misunderstanding of historical events and chronologies.

This American effort just confirmed the effects already taking hold in Germany and surely other nations immersed in viewing the same big budget historical films. The varied negotiations, where traditional history brushed shoulders with film, also showcased just how much historicism reigned as the guiding mode of thought toward the past. Yet, historical film provided the opportunity to experience the past in the rhythm and speed of the times, to update history. The sight-oriented transmission of historical information came in a form most closely resembling "daily life" and the historical imagination. Educators would need to follow the youth in this regard. This was expressed in the assertion made in 1926 that teachers of history need to "acquire the habit of mind that will enable [them] to think in the medium of pictures from the ground up."[89] The qualitative sense of the past and society's relationship to it seemed to shift rather than people really "knowing" more or less about history. As institutions adapted a variety of filmed histories into lectures, field trips, and essay topics students took on a uniquely modern relationship to the past alongside historicism. The institutional attempts to negotiate film as history lent some credibility to the slew of films being made. However, in shaping a sense of the past, the machine of the cinema industry would quickly surpass official instruction.

The Illusion of History

Like classical cinema, teachers often shaped a "*fixation on congruity*" which regulates [viewers'] assessment of detail and ensures [they] do not get it wrong and stumble into alternative, incongruous readings."[90] Instructors felt that child-like audiences required this discipline. However, the deep tension between historical film and history might be better served by a counter conception of children as subjects of reception. Working from the child's engagement with the world, Walter Benjamin offered just such a notion, scattered throughout his texts and fragments but formulated most extensively in the late 1920s.

Benjamin's children are "primitive" and "barbaric" in their relation to images, objects, their surroundings, and film. And it is precisely through their "miscognition," or playful misunderstanding/misappropriation, that children harbor a revolutionary potential. For this reason, "[i]n Benjamin's writing, the child plays a central role in an enchanting/disenchanting—that is, dialectic—treatment of history" toward "an intimacy with history and things that are strange."[91] This mode of reception more closely imagines the kind of interaction youth (and wider audience demographics) had with historical film. Explicitly against the reform and "colonial pedagogy" of Weimar, Benjamin advocated the promotion and fostering of children's creativity, imagination, and spontaneity.[92] With these traits, audiences, like children, could make their own meanings of historical images or even productively misunderstand them (in adult's terms). This consideration helps to remind us that there always exists a gap between authorial intent, as packaged messages, and the movie that ultimately plays in the heads of viewers.[93]

If the colonial pedagogy sought to teach borders and an ideological cartography of the world, it had to cultivate a regulated sense of nations and colonies. Similarly, historical instruction had to maintain the "unnatural" thinking that is historicism through its own disciplinary constructions. As Samuel Wineburg highlights, historicist thinking is an unnatural and entirely *learned* mode of thinking that requires a critical distance to the past.[94] Historicist thinking works against natural thought, which is often based on lived experience. As the term "availability heuristic" entails, humankind inherently bears an instinctual tendency for preferring and referring to (personal) experience as more easily available than statistical or verifiable data. Even in the presence of empirical evidence, "we are biased in the way we process evidence, making use of information that jumps out with the greatest vividness … often choosing what is most available over what is most trustworthy."[95] This was precisely what Weimar history teachers wanted their students to unlearn.

By filtering historical films through thinking in periods, eras, chronology, and political structures the youth would certainly learn history, but only as it is aimed at the expense of film's inherently wide "space for play."[96] Children's undisciplined reception of film is perhaps less desirable, but more natural than historical thinking because "the ways in which children perceive, organize, and interact" with their surroundings can "upset hierarchies" and current configurations."[97] This slippage between signs and meanings, as between temporalities, was not conducive to educational programs or historicist thinking. For most psychologists and pedagogues, children required guidance to counteract their undisciplined relationship to images and their surroundings.[98] Yet, for Benjamin the childlike approach bears potential precisely because it is linked to motor and sensory development and its miscognition can upset current constructions—even historiographical ones.

Benjamin encapsulated this productive miscognition in the image of a child grasping for the moon. As empty attempts, even failed revolutions have merit, since "just as a child learns to grasp by stretching out his hand for the moon as it would for a ball, so humanity, in its efforts at innervation, sets its sights as much on presently utopian goals as on goals within reach." But Benjamin's image of the child entails the unique historical juncture of having one's "*organs* in the second technology." Like the 1902 Edison short, *Uncle Josh at the Moving Picture Show*, where Josh interacts with the screen and ultimately penetrates the image by punching through the projection, the grasping at the unobtainable object entails a sensory instruction. The Edison short stages the very act of "improper" spectatorship for cinema audiences, and thus instructs through Josh's vicarious (and misguided) working through the image.

Similarly, the childlike act of misunderstanding or misperceiving the moon holds a utopian value for Benjamin. Miriam Hansen explains, "[t] he child's gesture may be based in motor-perceptual miscognition; but for Benjamin (unlike Piaget or Lacan, for instance), this miscognition fuels creative and transformative energies, anticipating an alternative organization of perception that would be equal to the technologically changed environment."[99] It is not whether that, which children create for themselves is illusion or real; in this Benjamin turns away from the developmental psychologists. As a creative and hopeful act, and simultaneously impossible and perhaps wrongheaded attempt, the child's reach innervates and instructs the embodied mind to reach and to grasp in general. While I am not arguing for the Marxist revolutionary potential of such miscognition, Benjamin's model and his counterintuitive interpretation nevertheless work as a telling metaphor for the relationship between audiences and historical film.

The educated trepidation (on the part of teachers and historians) concerning students' "misunderstanding" or miscognition of film images, as representations of the past parallel the (verifiable) insinuation that the moon is not graspable but that a ball is. The normative instruction and properly critical historical thinking treats the craft of the historian as more akin to reaching for a ball that can be properly grasped. However, what is implicit in the child's grasping for the moon and taking history films on in their own intimate and experiential way is that the past and the study of it are much more like reaching for the moon anyway.[100] That all history is a stretch, a constructed grasp at an ungraspable, only-mediated object, suffuses the more natural and unlearned approach to history on film that pedagogues were at pains to quell.

In fostering room for play in children's misrecognition, historical film enacts (while shaping) a cinematic sense of the past. It is precisely the effects of Stapel's "habituation" to the filmic medium that has resulted in a qualitative positive gain in historical consciousness. With the shift in *physis* from Homo Sapiens to some hybrid "homo cinematicus" the body and mind are engaged in history in a new and not merely degenerative way. Extending audiences' habituation to history on film into the present Vivian Sobchack has recognized that, "[i]mmersed in a culture in which the proliferation of visual representations has accelerated and understanding of 'textuality' has become pervasive, perpetually confronted with contestation between competing representational claims and forms, filmgoers have become unprecedentedly savvy about (mis)representation and have learned the lessons of Hayden White's *Metahistory* even if they've never read it."[101] The construction of this new sense of history, this new subjectivity toward the historical past, should remind one of Benjamin's more general hopes for the medium of film, as a means of coping with modernity.

Historical film instructs audiences in a modern sense of "textuality," that circumvents the reflective tendency to become mired in the aporia presented by constructivism. As a type of miscognition, this sense of textuality has long since attended the love and immersive enjoyment of history films. It is the equivalent to knowingly "stretching out [a] hand for the moon as [one] would for a ball," while realizing it will never be a ball. In such a mode, student viewers of history films have, across time, ranked film high for level of enjoyment and preference and very low for validity as historical narratives. It is no wonder that in their surveys of the mid 1990s among European fourteen- and fifteen-year-olds, researchers found that "[f]ictional films are the most favoured presentation of history with respect to enjoyment. Students in all countries like this kind of presentation." However, when asked how much they trust fictional films "[t]he overall average indicates that students are not really convinced of the reliability of fictional films. They trust them less than any other medium mentioned except 'historical novels'."[102]

Already in the 1920s, students and critics harbored skepticism toward history on film all while praising the experience. An important sense of the constructedness of the past resides in this relationship to history films. As a vernacular schooling in textuality, historical films stage the discrepancy between the moon and a ball. While preferring the form, students have generally always known the content is not "as it actually was." They have known the images on screen are both true and *always* false. Audiences of historical film have ever been at once consumers and students because they always want "to be fooled and at the same time nobody's fools, to oscillate, swing from knowledge to belief, from distance to adhesion, from criticism to fascination."[103]

Whether educational films in classrooms, "authentic" recreations, or Lubitsch international hits, all these films were implicated in a much larger project. The past represented on screen conditioned a view toward meaning and experience and "in favoring the visual and emotional data while simultaneously playing down the analytical" the films were already shifting the "very sense of the past."[104] Together with many other interconnected countries, Weimar Germany began to build and consume the history it wanted—a history that shaped and was shaped by an affective cinematic experience. Filmic constructions were ethically charged mediations of history raising hope and suspicion. As both manufactured documents and fictional portrayals in space and time, the film industry's creations manufactured the past for students and society alike. As Kurt Pinthus wrote of the same ancient Egyptian film set, visited by the many students and teachers, Egypt "the land, where the Pharaohs flourished ... do you know this land? We didn't know it—and couldn't travel there; but Lubitsch, the relentlessly hardworking one simply built it in the Märkisch deserts, with palaces and temples and the legendary city of Thebes, with people, a king, and priests."[105] Like an unfulfilled reach for the moon, Lubitsch, his crew, and their numerous audiences reached out to grasp an unattainable ancient past, as a playful present construction.

Notes

1 L. Kreiselmeier, *Schulkinematographie. Der Film in Schule, Jugendpflege, Verein und Heim* (Union Deutsche Verlag, 1925), 12.
2 "Die Lubitsch-Filmstadt," *Der Kinematograph* 774, December 18, 1921.
3 Philip Rosen, *Change Mummified: Cinema, Historicity, Theory* (Minneapolis, MN: University of Minnesota Press, 2001), 254–55.
4 Emilie Altenloh, "A Sociology of the Cinema: The Audience," *Screen* 42, no. 3 (September 21, 2001): 279.
5 Colin Heywood, *A History of Childhood: Children and Childhood in the West from Medieval to Modern Times* (Hoboken, NJ: John Wiley & Sons, 2013), 3.
6 Barbara Hanke, *Geschichtskultur an höheren Schulen von der Wilhelminischen Ära bis zum Zweiten Weltkrieg: Das Beispiel Westfalen* (Germany: LIT Verlag Münster, 2011), 105.
7 H. G. Wells, *The Idea of A League of Nations* (Boston: Atlantic Monthly Press, 1919), 8.
8 Hanke, *Geschichtskultur an höheren Schulen*, 123.
9 Robert A. Rosenstone, *Visions of the Past: The Challenge of Film to Our Idea of History* (Cambridge, MA: Harvard University Press, 1995), 36.
10 Robert A. Rosenstone, "History in Images/History in Words: Reflections on the Possibility of Really Putting History onto Film," *The American Historical Review* 93, no. 5 (December 1, 1988): 1177.

11 Theodor W. Adorno and Henry W. Pickford, *Critical Models: Interventions and Catchwords* (New York: Columbia University Press, 2005), 55.

12 Marnie Hughes-Warrington, *The History on Film Reader* (London: Routledge, 2009), 5.

13 Ibid.

14 Vivian Sobchack, "The Insistent Fringe: Moving Images and Historical Consciousness," *History and Theory* 36, no. 4 (December 1, 1997): 5.

15 See for instance Droop, *Kinematographie im Unterricht der Geschichte* and Scholz, *Geschichte um Lichtbilde*, both from 1913 and Oskar Kalbus, *Der Deutsche Lehrfilm in Der Wissenschaft Und Im Unterricht* (Berlin, 1922, 1922), 161.

16 This is evidenced in attitudes toward music as well, see Holly Watkins, *Metaphors of Depth in German Musical Thought: From E. T. A. Hoffmann to Arnold Schoenberg* (Cambridge, MA: Cambridge University Press, 2011), 22–25.

17 Hanke, *Geschichtskultur an höheren Schulen*, 105.

18 Frederick William Roman, *The New Education in Europe* (London: Routledge and Sons, 1923), 196.

19 Hanke, *Geschichtskultur an höheren Schulen*, 105.

20 Ibid.

21 Roman, *The New Education in Europe*, 196.

22 Siegfried Kawerau, *Synoptische Tabellen Für Den Geschichtlichen Arbeits-Unterricht Vom Ausgang Des Mittelalters Bis Zur Gegenwart* (Berlin: F. Schneider, 1921), iii.

23 Ibid., v.

24 Knut Engeler, *Geschichtsunterricht und Reformpädagogik* (Berlin: LIT Verlag Münster, 2009), 59.

25 Walter Schoenbrunn, "Geschichtsunterricht" *Welt-Bühne* 17 (1921): 641.

26 Engeler, *Geschichtsunterricht und Reformpädagogik*, 61.

27 Ibid., 133.

28 Hanke, *Geschichtskultur an höheren Schulen*, 125.

29 Engeler, *Geschichtsunterricht und Reformpädagogik*, 51.

30 Gustav Würtenberg, "Geschichtsunterricht und Kino," *Vergangenheit und Gegenwart* 18, no. 6 (1928): 362.

31 Kalbus, *Der Deutsche Lehrfilm*, 23.

32 "Zur Einführung," *Bild Archiv* 1 (1920): 1.

33 Siegfried Kracauer "Photography," in *The Mass Ornament: Weimar Essays* (Cambridge: Harvard University Press, 1995), 51.

34 *Bild-Archiv* 8 (1920): 2.

35 Erwin Ackerknecht, *Das Lichtspiel im Dienste der Bildungspflege: Handbuch für Lichtspielreformer* (Berlin: Weidmann, 1918), 58.

36 Ibid., 36.

37 Ibid., 54.

38 Karl Gentil, "Lehrfilm—Beiprogrammfilm," *Der Kinematograph* 739, 1920.

39 Thomas Elsässer and Michael Wedel, *A Second Life: German Cinema's First Decades* (Amsterdam: Amsterdam University Press, 1996), 193.

40 Dr. von Leszel, "Die Berliner Urania und der Kulturfilm," in *Das Kulturfilmbuch*, ed. E. Beyfuss and A. Kossowsky (Berlin: Carl P. Chryselius'scher Verlag, 1924), 338.

41 *New York Times*, July 10, 1925, 17.

42 Konrad Lange, *Das Kino in Gegenwart und Zukunft* (Stuttgart: Enke, 1920), 89.

43 Rosen, *Change Mummified*, 157.

44 Sol Cohen, "An Innocent Eye: The 'Pictorial Turn,' Film Studies, and History," *History of Education Quarterly* 43, no. 2 (July 1, 2003): 254.

45 James Jacob Lizska, *General Introduction to the Semiotic of Charles Sanders Peirce* (Bloomington, IL: Indiana University Press, 1996), 37–38.

46 Hugo Münsterberg, *The Photoplay: A Psychological Study* (New York: Appleton, 1916), 27.

47 William Urrichio, "*The Kulturfilm*: A Brief History of an Early Discursive Practice," in *Prima di Caligari: cinema tedesco, 1895–1920*, Paolo Cherchi Usai et al. (Edizioni Biblioteca dell'immagine, 1990), 358.

48 See Naldo Felke, "Cinema's Damaging Effects on Health," in *The Promise of Cinema*, Anton Kaes, Nicholas Baer, and Michael Cowan, eds., (Berkeley: CA: University of California Press, 2016), 234–35.

49 Wilhelm Stapel, "Der Homo Cinematicus," in *The Promise of Cinema*, Anton Kaes, Nicholas Baer, and Michael Cowan, eds., (Berkeley: CA: University of California Press, 2016), 243.

50 Nicholas Carr, "Is Google Making Us Stupid?," *The Atlantic*, July–August 2008, 56–63.

51 Nicholas Carr, *The Shallows: What the Internet Is Doing to Our Brains* (New York: W. W. Norton & Company, 2011), 3.

52 "*Madame Dubarry* in Amerika," *Lichtbild-Bühne* 46 (November 13, 1920): 20.

53 Dr. Ernst Seeger, "Staat und Kulturfilm" in E. Beyfuss, *Das Kulturfilmbuch*, ed. E. Beyfuss (Berlin: Carl P. Chryselius'scher Verlag, 1924), 74–75.

54 Ackerknecht, *Das Lichtspiel im Dienste der Bildungspflege* (Berlin: Weidmannsche Buchhandlung, 1918), 52, 60.

55 Paul Eller, "Geschichtsstudium und Film," *Der Kinematograph* 752, 1921.

56 Gotthold Ephraim Lessing, *Laokoon, Oder, Über Die Grenzen Der Malerei Und Poesie: Studienausgabe*, Reclams Universal-Bibliothek Nr. 18865 (Stuttgart: Reclam, [1766] 2012).

57 W. J. T. Mitchell and Mark B. N. Hansen, *Critical Terms for Media Studies* (Chicago: University of Chicago Press, 2010), 93.

58 Sabine Hake, *German National Cinema* (London: Routledge, 2008), 40; Stephen Kern, *The Culture of Time and Space, 1880–1918: With a New Preface*, 2nd ed. (Cambridge, MA: Harvard University Press, 2003), 6.

59 Wulf Köpke, *The Critical Reception of Alfred Döblin's Major Novels* (Rochester, NY: Camden House, 2003), 133.

60 Therese Fischer-Seidel, "Archetypal Structures and Literature in Joyce's *Ulysses*: Aristotle, Frye, and the Plot of Ulysses," in *Self-Reflexivity in Literature*, eds. Werner Huber, Martin Middeke, and Hubert Zapf (Germany: Königshausen & Neumann, 2005), 94.

61 James Joyce, *Ulysses* (London: Oxford University Press, 1998), 37.

62 Kuno Fischer, *Geschichte der neuern philosophie* (Heidelberg: F. Bassermann, 1869), 316.

63 Svetlana Boym, *The Future of Nostalgia* (New York: Basic Books, 2001), 9–10.

64 Maurice Merleau-Ponty and Talia Welsh, *Child Psychology and Pedagogy: The Sorbonne Lectures 1949–1952* (Evanston, IL: Northwestern University Press, 2010).

65 Similarly mentioned in "Auge und Film," *Der Kinematograph*, 756, 1921.

66 Ackerknecht, *Das Lichtspiel im Dienste der Bildungspflege*, 52.

67 Hannu Salmi "Film as Historical Narration," *Film-Historia* 5, no. 1 (1995): 45.

68 Gustav Benkwitz, "Geschichtsstudium und Film," *Der Kinematograph* 756, 1921.

69 Paul Eller, "Geschichtsstudium und Film: Eine Entgegnung," *Der Kinematograph* 758, 1921.

70 Hayden White, "Historiography and Historiophoty," *The American Historical Review* 93, no. 5 (December 1, 1988): 1193–99.

71 Rosen, *Change Mummified*, 242.

72 Ibid., 245.

73 Robert A. Rosenstone and Constantin Parvulescu, *A Companion to the Historical Film* (Hoboken, NJ: John Wiley & Sons, 2012), 2.

74 Fritz Lang, "Kitsch–Sensation–Kultur–und Film," in *Das Kulturfilmbuch*, ed. E. Beyfuss and A. Kossowsky (Berlin: Carl P. Chryselius'scher Verlag, 1924), 28.

75 Peter Seixas, "Young People's Understanding of the History of Native–White Relations," in *Celluloid Blackboard: Teaching History with Film*, ed. Alan S. Marcus (Charlotte: Information Age Publishing, 2006), 108–9.

76 David Wark Griffith, *The Rise and Fall of Free Speech in America* (Los Angeles, CA, 1916 [no publisher]).

77 Johannes Molzahn, "Stop Reading! Look!" in *The Weimar Republic Sourcebook*, ed. Martin Jay, Anton Kaes, Edward Dimendberg (Oakland, CA: University of California Press, 1995), 648–49.

78 Helen Marot, "The Creative and Efficiency Concepts in Education," *Dial* (April 11, 1918): 341–44.

79 Paul Eller, "Geschichtsstudium und Film," *Der Kinematograph* 752, 1921.

80 "Der Lehrfilm in den Preussischen Schulen," *Deutsche Lichtspiel-Zeitung*, 18 (1920): 4.

81 See Chapter 2 herein.

82 Donald J. Mattheisen, "Filming U.S. History during the 1920S: The Chronicles of America Photoplays," *Historian* 54, no. 4 (June 1, 1992): 627–40.

83 *Der Kinematograph*, 775.

84 "100 Reels of History," *Film Daily*, no. 20 (January 21, 1922): 2.

85 "The Chronicles of America Photoplays," *The Metropolitan Museum of Art Bulletin* 20, no. 7 (July 1, 1925): 186.

86 Mattheisen, "Filming U.S. History during the 1920S," 630.

87 Daniel C. Knowlton and J. Warren Tilton, *Motion Pictures in History Teaching* (Motion Pictures in History Teaching, (New Haven: Yale University Press, 1929), 93.

88 Ibid.

89 Nathaniel Stephenson, "The Goal of the Motion Picture in Education," *Annals of the American Academy of Political and Social Science*, vol. 128 of *The Motion Picture in Its Economic and Social Aspects* (November 1926): 119.

90 Christian Keathley, *Cinephilia and History, or, the Wind in the Trees* (Bloomington: Indiana University Press, 2006) 42.

91 Nicola Gess, "Gaining Sovereignty: On the Figure of the Child in Walter Benjamin's Writing," *MLN* 125, no. 3 (2010): 682–708.

92 Miriam Bratu Hansen, *Cinema and Experience: Siegfried Kracauer, Walter Benjamin, and Theodor W. Adorno* (Oakland, CA: University of California Press, 2011), 184.

93 Günter Riederer, "Film und Geschichtswissenschaft," in *Visual History*, ed. Gerhard Paul (Germany: Vandenhoeck & Ruprecht, 2006), 96, 97.

94 Samuel S. Wineburg, *Historical Thinking and Other Unnatural Acts: Charting the Future of Teaching the Past* (Philadelphia, PA: Temple University Press, 2001).

95 Samuel S. Wineburg, "Unnatural and Essential: The Nature of Historical Thinking," *Teaching History* 129 (December 2007): 7.

96 Walter Benjamin, *The Work of Art in the Age of Its Technological Reproducibility, and Other Writings on Media*, ed. Michael W. Jennings, Brigid Doherty, and Thomas Y. Levin, 1st ed. (Cambridge, MA: Belknap Press, 2008).

97 Hansen, *Cinema and Experience*, 149.

98 Walter Benjamin, Michael William Jennings, and Rodney Livingstone, *Walter Benjamin* (Cambridge, MA: Harvard University Press, 2005), 251.

99 Hansen, *Cinema and Experience*, 143.

100 In an unpublished fragment Benjamin emphasized the point that "memory is not an instrument for exploring the past but rather a medium." Michael William Jennings, and Rodney Livingstone, *Walter Benjamin* (Cambridge: Harvard University Press, 2005), 576.

101 Sobchack, "The Insistent Fringe," 5.

102 *Youth and History: A Comparative European Survey on Historical Consciousness and Political Attitudes Among Adolescents* (Hamburg: Körber-Stiftung, 1997), A 86. (This sentiment is also duplicated in Marcus, Paxton, Meyerson, "The Reality of It All," History Students Read the Movies," *Theory and Research in Social Education* 34, no. 3 (2006): 540).

103 Jean-Louis Comolli, "Historical Fiction: A Body Too Much?" reprinted in Hughes-Warrington, *The History on Film Reader*, 68.

104 Rosenstone, "History in Images/History in Words," 1179.

105 Kurt Pinthus, "Lubitsch in Ägypten," *Das Tage-Buch* 11 (March 18, 1922): 417.

4 Clio in Crisis

"History is a scenario and a play, a swiftly moving film and a drama in which every human passion contends with every other, brutally or intellectually, upon the stage of life."

—Franklin Giddings, 1920.[1]

Historical practices were undergoing swift change. The craft of the historian seemed to require updating, possibly even reconceptualization. Unfortunately, German historian and theologian Ernst Troeltsch was never able to complete his rigorous study of historicism's problematic nature. Originally conceived as two volumes, only the first, *Der Historismus und Seine Probleme*, ever came to fruition. His sudden death on February 1, 1923 also left a scheduled series of lectures to be delivered in England equally unfulfilled.[2] Troeltsch's personal efforts to rekindle the philosophy of history signaled hope for History in crisis, but fizzled with his passing. Adolf von Harnack, fellow professor of theology and church history, offered the honorary address at Troeltsch's funeral. In the grim presence of Troeltsch's lifeless body, Harnack summoned the aspiration of his colleague's project by quoting the last words of *Der Historismus*. This citation was, in Harnack's eyes, Troeltsch's last will and testament. The final passage of the incomplete work reads, "In order to complete the great task of formulating a new philosophy of history, confident and courageous men are needed, not skeptics or mystics, not rationalistic fanatics and not omniscient historians … the task itself which consciously or unconsciously presented itself to every historical epoch is particularly pressing for our moment of life."[3]

Reading the excerpt as he did, Harnack implicitly coupled the death of Troeltsch with a nearly futile attempt to redeem nineteenth-century historicism in crisis. Troeltsch himself had already recognized that the very "logic and epistemological theory of historical thought had given way."[4] A new philosophy of history would have to eschew any delusion of omniscience. Of course, the ultimate project of Troeltsch's intellectual wrestling was to somehow neither do away with historicism nor slip into pure relativism. His cryptic hope was to "overcome history by history."[5] In other words, history would surely continue as long as "Geschichte" survived—as a construction of the past through "the modalities of memory and hope"[6]—yet the crisis rendered a fatal blow to historiography's authority and sheen of objectivity, spiraling these into the inevitable realm of relativity. Historicism's inherent problems had finally culminated in a "crisis," requiring a solution.

The precarious loss of stability was not confined to historical thought. The foundations of mathematics, physics, and science in general were likewise shaken. The waxing sense of crisis had its own history and came to a head, permeating academic thought, during the Weimar Republic. In fact, "[t]he whole period of German thought from 1880 to 1930 is almost incomprehensible without an awareness of this crisis-mentality afflicting both the natural and the human sciences."[7] The crisis was even felt in grade school history teaching.

Würtenberg included the urgency of crisis in his advocacy for implementing motion pictures in historical instruction. "The problem of *Historismus*, the question of 'history and life' is for us all a significant moment in the general cultural crisis of our time, an affliction, under which we all suffer."[8] Würtenberg hoped the power of film could be utilized to counter the effects of a shattered historical authority. By updating historical thought, while appealing to students' emotions and desires, film had something to offer historical practice. Würtenberg's concrete hope that film could somehow rescue historicism from its plight was echoed on a theoretical level.

The potential of cinema in the face of historical skepticism sparked "new" historical work and theory. Because of intellectual and technological developments, early Weimar was a defining moment along the trajectories of historical studies and the fostering of history on film. It was at this point that the two practices crossed with some important discursive interaction. Thus, while the recognition and naming of the "crisis of historicism," embodied in Troeltsch, might seem, at first glance, entirely disconnected from the developments and repercussions of film they actually converged in productive ways. As the widespread nineteenth-century iteration of historicism became, like Troeltsch himself, sick and old, efforts to rethink the historian's craft were galvanized through the influence of film and photography.

Clearly, historical films (widely transmitting literal images of the past) influenced and even standardized, to some degree, mental images of the past for international audiences. However, this chapter sharpens a different focus by pursuing the intersection of film and historical thought in at least two interrelated ways. First, this chapter reveals how certain films "featured" the crisis of historicism: the relativity of views of the past, demands for new history, and ruptures in historical traditions through form and content. Connected with the first claim, I argue that the escalation of cinema's reach and influence affected the writing of historical literature and thought, resulting in the adoption of imagistic and formal features borrowed from film. Taken as a pair, these two imbricated developments disclose the reaction to widespread notions of crisis and the effects of a "new" media landscape for history.

Photographic media helped to emphasize, as it did for Benjamin, "the question of the image at the problematic center of modernity."[9] Historical images and representation were modernized in form and technological reproducibility. For Benjamin's contemporary and interlocutor, Siegfried Kracauer, film also served as a figural filter for historical thought. These two theorists, perhaps best, represent early attempts to revitalize (innervate) the craft of history through media-theoretical ingenuity. Although they were not alone, they went beyond reform pedagogy or the movement of "New History," while partaking of the same fervor for updating historical thought. Their insightful coupling of historiography and film was the result of both author's keen observations of the shifting medial and historical landscapes around them, where film could decisively change history.

Film came to influence history by packaging and selling a new type of historical representation, one that engaged bodies and more closely reflected the modern age. By the mid-1920s, many consumed the majority of their historical experiences in the cinemas. This media revolution, where film shaped historical thought, did not create the crisis of historicism, nor did it solve it. Yet, the deeply felt problematic informed "historical" productions of both individual films as well as film-inspired thought and writing. Together these forms engaged with the crisis of historicism and helped to translate it into culturally consumed terms.

Historical Thought in Film

Historicism was born and bred by writing. Any occurrence before the invention of writing was, for Schiller, "as good as lost to world history."[10] It was the very act of writing that brought the past into sequence and coherence for the present. However, historicism's reliance on the medium of writing for both its source material and composition was challenged by technological advancements, especially those that could record. Photography, phonography, telegraphy, and cinematography created "truer" sources, while eschewing the human chronicler. Along with its ability to record, cinema offered new possibilities for historical representation. Screen histories echoed the modern experience of time and space and could play fast and loose with chronology and proximity. By capturing duration and then projecting edited and compiled source material in narrative form, film exploded the act of history. Some films seemed to realize this before historians did.

As a democratic form, film provided a format to popularly and visually register the crisis of historicism. Reflecting, while shaping, a modern sense of temporality, film worked history into a cinematic temporality. The technology of cinema could circumvent, even subvert, the causal and linear structure of nineteenth-century historiography. Some films, like *Der Müde Tod* (1921) seemed to respond structurally and by deliberately infusing the cinematic form with philosophical aspirations.[11] Working against the chronologic of historicism, *Der Müde Tod*, *Das Wachsfigurenkabinett* (1924), and *Intolerance* (1916) equally employed repetitive structures, plotting the same actors in overlapping historical periods and places. This effect was also happening across films. As Ernst Lubitsch's three major historical films enacted, Emil Jannings was King Louis XV, then King Henry VIII, and lastly Pharaoh Amenes. Taken in a series, these roles repeated the effect toyed with in individual "frame films" with parallel storylines. The repeated actors on screen broke through the temporal constraints of progressive time and positivism. Although the films were projected from beginning to end, the structure allowed for deep temporal disjuncture. Time and space on screen became reversible, recurring, and technologically representable. Audiences were increasingly experiencing history as a vision presented to them with its own logic of continuity and display.

Visualizing the placement of a modern subject into multiple historical contexts worked against the temporalization of the past perpetuated by nineteenth-century historicism. The form of repetition surfaced like the return of historicism's repressed past. The renewed interest in premodern, cyclical, recurring, and fictional portrayals of the past seemed fitting in the modern medium of film. At the very least, the cyclical layering of history films offered a deviation from standard historical narration, but it also allowed figures to enter a time period that was not their own, even within the film's own diegetic world. Various times and places could be cut together into collision or instructive integration and human agents could visually step into the past.

Some films even staged the very (self-reflexive) act of projecting history cinematically, by showing historical thought as a film within the film. By making historical thought, a cinematic display, these films literalized the often neglected part of White's formulation of "historiophoty," which is literally history written in light, but also the visual "representation of history and *our thought about it.*"[12] As a medium for historical thought, cinema could represent thinking about the past in influential ways. While history films were already in the thick of presenting the historical display, it is perhaps not surprising that films visualizing historical thought as a film could come from outside the genre. The enlightenment film *Anders als die Andern* (1919) and the other expressionistic proto-horror film *Der Golem* (1919) both displayed historical thought as cinematic. As outliers these films could be more experimental in form and portray historical thought on a meta-level. Often the historical thought on film made it a shared, even if supremely personal, take on a given past. A moving instance of this occurs early in Richard Oswald's *Anders als die Andern* (1919) when the protagonist, Paul Körner, stops the narrative flow to visualize his own counter-history.

Körner sits dejectedly reading the morning news. Here the information of old media sparks the potential of new media. Enacting the parallel structure of *Intolerance*, Körner "senses a common thread" and, in a flash of revelatory thought, links the current news of inexplicable suicides in the newspaper with past homosexual men. The historical figures in Körner's mind hail from varying periods and places but, as the current news of male suicides implies, all suffered under legally sanctioned intolerance. Körner's personal vision brings a historical element to the film, which functions as a treatise against the official ban on homosexual activity found in paragraph 175 of the German penal code. The past invades the present. "In his mind's eye," Körner visualizes history as a procession of prominent figures that are either persecuted or unacknowledged homosexuals. Because of the new historical medium, the audience is made privy to his mental image of that historical collection. Without the necessity of dialogue or writing, the film transmits a new and visual mode of history.

Ironically, this symptomatic illustration of cinematic historical thought has been lost to history. The only remaining image of the important segment in the fragmentary extant film is a still photo of the sumptuously adorned figures. The group includes "Peter Tchaikovsky, Leonardo da Vinci, Oscar Wilde, King Friedrich II of Prussia, and King Ludwig II of Bavaria" standing in procession under a banner with "§ 175" written on it. As Hansen has argued of *Intolerance*'s structural power, *Anders*, in this brief moment, also "harks back to earlier instances of parallelism ... in which the parallel construction was geared towards a conceptual point, an argument of social, political, and aesthetic nature."[13] *Anders*, as a contemporary social commentary in 1919, utilizes a radical historical vision to sharpen its edge. The effect renders the scene not only good metacinema, but great metahistory.

The form of *Intolerance* allows the film to momentarily instruct the audience in thinking historically by envisioning the past cinematically. Several of the historical personages displayed seem to even visually prefigure subjects in Oswald's own period films such as *Lady Hamilton* (1921), *Lucrezia Borgia* (1922), and *Carlos und Elisabeth* (1923). Oswald then took his own protagonist's cue of cinematic historical thinking and bounced between "enlightenment films," aimed at social improvement, and historical pieces that bridged all humans everywhere. For it was Oswald who proclaimed, "to only show humanity in a universally understandable form, is the deepest and most excellent mission of the historical film."[14] This use of the "mind's eye" empowers audiences with empathic historical vision, by enacting the same, while revealing the role of film in structuring historical thought and making the outcome collective.

If *Anders* instrumentalized *Intolerance*'s antihistoricist structure then Paul Wegener's *Der Golem* (1919) literalized the diplomatic act of sharing history visually, by rendering subjective historical vision as an objectively seen collective experience. During a visit to the royal court, the Rabbi Loew has his living clay Golem creation stand at the rear of the room. From the front of the hall, the Rabbi proceeds to project his people's "patriarchs" as a cinematic illusion for his Christian audience, as if radiating from the imposing Golem at the rear. Beyond his spatial relationship to the audience in the room, the Golem further reflects a cinema projector with his rolled up scroll tucked neatly into his chest.

As a cinematic display meant to ease the tension between Jew and Gentile, the Rabbi's projection carries extraordinary potential. But the Rabbi's historical film requires an attentive and seated audience. Only those willing to conform to the appropriate practice of spectatorship are permitted to view the historical images flashing against the wall. The spectators are told to sit still and not "laugh or speak." The Rabbi's attempt to bridge Jewish and Gentile worlds through sharing visual history unfortunately fails as the onlookers begin to snicker and their growing laughter literally brings down the house. Amid crumbling architecture and a fatal fire, both projector and projectionist must make a run for it. Although a failed attempt, the scene shows historical thinking as filmic images and equally makes clear society's relatively new ability to visually share historical thoughts as collective memories.

The shared historical thought in both *Anders* and *Der Golem* offer counter-histories by displaying marginal and persecuted peoples. As film instructed audiences on how to visualize the past and make it a collective experience it fostered the exploration of otherwise unfamiliar or overlooked aspects of the past, a feature that also came to inspire historiography.

Film in Historical Thought

Despite its inherent residence in the present tense, film was a powerful medium in portraying, while shaping, historical thought. Film functioned like Sir Walter Scott's historical novels for Leopold von Ranke,[15] or Bilderbögen and historical anecdotes for Theodor Fontane.[16] These sources and media informed (by rejection and incorporation) not only the content but also the form of both men's individual historical thinking. As the historical novel had provided a productive counterpoint for historicism in the nineteenth century,[17] film offered a new possible model at the turn of the century. In his review of Lubitsch's *Das Weib des Pharao* in 1922, Alfred Kerr already realized the connection. He wrote, "[i]t is peculiar how film in its own way repeats literary history. The historical novel stood earlier in full bloom. The historical film is now reaching its pinnacle."[18] Yet, the photographic medium challenged traditional historiography more directly—and demographically much more broadly—than literature had.

As a dynamic, and thoroughly modern, means of communication, the medium exercised influence on the writing of history. The medium helped some historians in crisis to reconceptualize the past and their work. After viewing scenes like those mentioned earlier it was not surprising that figurations of historical vision evolved in description from the "stage of world events,"[19] in the eighteenth and nineteenth centuries to the processional "film"[20] of history in the twentieth century. When Kant, Schelling, Hegel, and Marx used the tradition of universal history as a dramatic world stage where certain "roles" are played the particular figuration already required certain updates. In order to secularize the Christian world theater, "'Nature,' 'Spirit' or 'production,' 'Mankind' or 'History'" t[ook] the place of God as director.[21] This rich legacy of history as a dramatic stage could easily slide into cinematic language and still retain the elements of scenes, conflicts between appearance and meaning, and the disciplinary hope for the visibility of history in action through imagination. However, with film the dramatic staging of personal/professional historical vision could be made public as a shared perspective.

Drama and film provided cultural ways to express and externalize internal, or mental, historical vision. Like the Rabbi's literalized historical projection in *Golem* portrays, "[w]henever we try to give an account of mental images, we seem compelled to resort to some external, material apparatus as the model for the mind–a theater or cinema, a *musée imaginaire*, a camera obscura, a computer, a camera."[22] The medium of film informed not only individual thoughts but also the representations of thought processes. Through the last three centuries, philosophers, scientists, and artists have continued a tradition of conceptualizing the human mind and vision through the optical media and technology that shaped their own sight and understanding.[23] Humans constantly internalize certain "images of media" as "subjective pictures of our own mental processes."[24] In the wake of cinema, historical thought and its representation followed suit.

When Kracauer stated in 1927 that Historicism was like "a giant film," it was more than mere idiosyncrasy.[25] The borrowing also surfaced three years earlier in American sociologist Franklin Giddings' "Theory of History." For Giddings prehistory was a "film of scenes rather than a play." Accordingly, Giddings' description starts with media metalanguage doubling the narrating historian as projectionist. "As the reel begins to move we see sluggish rivers, and tropical trees alive with monkeys …." This narration continues through-out: "[n]ow on the screen come bones …" finally concluding, "with one more scene the film of prehistory ends."[26]

Film critic and practitioner Béla Balázs wrote of the past as events that "do not pass away, but like 'motionless soul-preserving pictures line up one behind the other (as if in the film)', and come alive when we recall them."[27] Balázs' proximity to the film industry yielded a more explicit connection. His conception of film as the medium that facilities human access to the past sounded something like James Joyce's statement that when he would close his eyes and lay down he would "see a cinematograph going on and on and it [would] bring[] back to [his] memory things [he] had almost forgot-ten."[28] From seemingly insignificant figural borrowings to rich interweaving of media, signs were surfacing that film had become a medium for thinking about the past.

Whether out of film envy, fear, optimistic excitement, or subconscious appropriation, intermedial borrowings from film helped to shape the form and process of historiography. This kind of cinematic influence on thought and writing is more easily discerned in modernist literature and has been treated elsewhere.[29] In fact, while reviewing James Joyce's *Ulysses*, German author, Alfred Döblin already recognized in 1928 that, "the cinema ha[d] penetrated the sphere of literature."[30] However, the formal interaction between film and historiography in the silent period has gone largely unno-ticed. Several historical writers bear this brushing with the medium. Yet, in response to the crisis of historicism and as outsiders to the discipline of history, Kracauer and Benjamin most explicitly and consciously engaged the prospect. The trend was not as advanced or widespread as it was in the late twentieth century when, "filmgoers and historians [had] become the same,"[31] but already in the interwar period, film and history—even histo-riography—were more entangled than most historians would have liked to concede.

The Need for New History

In response to the pervasive crises of modernity and historicism, Benjamin and Kracauer both borrowed from the medium of the film to rethink his-tory and historiography. Although they had very little positive to say about individual history films, they nevertheless exhibit the cinematic mode of historical thought portrayed in the films mentioned earlier. Both authors' turn to historical method should be seen in constellation with not only the crisis of historicism in Germany, but also with its wider manifestation internationally in trends seeking to reconsider the craft of the historian.

Therefore, a panoramic shot of their historical milieu is helpful before focusing on their more radical filmic writing. Among this postwar reappraisal of history, where even historians like Otto Hintze's "views were turned upside down,"[32] one might include Benedetto Croce's call for "New Historiography" in his influential work on methodology and historical theory in 1921, the international reform pedagogy movements treated in Chapter 3, and the Anglophone desire, engendered by the so-called Columbia School, to rewrite the past for the present and advance the style and merit of what they termed "New History." This last effort captured and spread much of the spirit of modern historiographical renewal.

The New History movement in America had its roots, like the epistemological crisis of history and the invention of motion pictures, in the late nineteenth century. Far from a monolithic body of practitioners or one singular movement, the term New History was thrown around in the early twentieth century as a vague label for stylistic changes in history writing and presentation, along with answers to a call for ways to reach and instruct the masses in all things historical. But Robinson most forcefully articulated the project in his 1912 publication, *New History: Essays Illustrating the Modern Historical Outlook*. Although not often remembered today, Robinson was "arguably the leading historian of his day" and incredibly influential, which helped legitimize the movement.[33]

Robinson was convinced that "New History" was "escaping the limitations formerly imposed upon the study of the past." The liberation of historiography for new historians meant widening the scope and ideals of history. Against the tradition of cataloguing, privileging political history, and focusing on the most conspicuous or sensational events, New History would forward a radical *relation* to the past. Because the "present ha[d] hitherto been the willing victim of the past," the new mode of writing would "turn on the past and exploit it in the interests of advance."[34] Robinson hoped history could catch up with the times and affect thinking on a higher plane. History would play its part in creating "*an unprecedented attitude of mind to cope with unprecedented conditions, and to utilize unprecedented knowledge.*"[35] Historians would acknowledge and even embrace the relative, constructed, and provisional nature of history, and seek to include more knowledge and methodology from neighboring disciplines. By relinquishing their former insularity, historians could forge a new tradition and radicalize the craft, wresting it from conservative control and antiquated tradition.

For new historians, the disorderly and disconnected past resembled more of a chaotic, inconsistent, and flowing stream of life. In a legitimate turn of presentism, the past's fragmentary state already seemed to correspond to modernity. The New History practitioners described the construction of the past much like a film—each frame containing overlooked items and ever in flux. "History should not be regarded as a stationary subject," as Robinson stated.[36] History is "not fixed and immutable, but ever changing ... [h]istory, from this point of view, may be regarded as an artificial extension and broadening of our memories."[37]

Yale Professor of History Daniel Knowlton explicitly correlated the spirit and focus of the New History with the medium of motion pictures in 1928. He argued that the sociological and new historical bend was parallel to the widespread "democratized" interest in mass psychology and film. The recognition that small "countless human factors" influenced the "whole of which they are a part" was tied to historical understanding and film convention. Knowlton explained that because of this "a tremendous impetus has been injected into the study of sociology which seeks to reveal the key to an understanding of the interrelationships of these human atoms."[38] In relating significance between the individual and the masses, as well as the common man and the ruling elite, New History was to enact the crosscutting of films that were achieving just such an effect visually. One might think of the skillful cutting between a close-up of an individual female followed by a long shot of the masses, of which she is a significant and formative part. This then characterized a "new conception of history" captured in the New History movement. Knowlton was convinced that "[t]he new history ha[d] at last found a most appropriate vehicle for its expression—the photoplay." By offering mass instruction, whereby audiences see themselves "mirrored in the acts of others,"[39] as individuals within modern masses, the medium of film most closely resembled the inclusive focus of New History.

Becker, a prominent historian at Cornell University and student of the new historians, wrote "the past is a kind of screen upon which each generation projects its vision of the future." For this reason, the "recurring phenomenon" of "new history" was ultimately a sign of "hope."[40] The entire notion of developing a "new history" was understood in terms of a medium. The most apt medium for Becker to turn to in conceptualizing the historian's craft and the state of historiography was film. History was simply a "projection" of current interests onto a "screen"—an effort to make the past useful for the present. Becker teased out another important aspect of history in crisis. Conceptions of the past had become screens as filters—our personal efforts to forget and construct only what we need. History for New History sounded more like memory. The medium of film sharpened the mediated aspect of historiography and helped historical theory mature.

Even hopeful historians acknowledged their anxiety that the rise of cinema as an institution offering narratives and experiences of the past was eclipsing historiography—turning readers into spectators. On July 7, 1925, Sir Charles Firth spoke at the "Annual Anglo-American conference of Professors of History." During this speech he lamented the "diminution in the number of readers of history." As a counterpoint to Firth's claims, the *New York Times* suggested that one need look no further than the recent publication of Wells', *Outline of History*.[41] In order to facilitate a wider readership, history should be rewritten and made "as interesting as Mr. Wells has done it," stated the columnist.[42] Troeltsch even validated the work by reviewing it in comparison with Oswald Spengler's *The Decline of the West*.[43] Troeltsch recognized the appeal of the *Outline of History*, although the outline was largely a product of Wells' mind and political agenda, at least Wells attempted to "exploit the past in the interest of advance" and write history aimed at mass audiences in more entertaining ways.[44] Even those who dismissed Wells' book as pseudohistory saw some potential in its publication.[45] Where many people were already accustomed to watching, at least Wells might help to inspire some to pick up a history book and read.[46]

The New History, in its methodological shift, also mirrored the inclusive element of historical thought visualized in films, where neglected elements were treated with care. New History widened the historiographical panorama by including previously overlooked subject matter. The new historian could research "a Roman villa or a primitive steam engine, or contrast the theology of Luther with that of St. Thomas Aquinas; he [could] trace the origin of Gothic architecture or of the Egyptian calendar, portray the infatuation of Henry VIII for Anne Boleyn, or Bismarck's attitude toward the socialists or the hatchets of Neolithic man."[47]

What might have earlier seemed merely marginal detritus of the past, like the incidentals in the background of a photograph, could in fact house dormant history. In this regard for quotidian elements, the New History already harbored some of the "cinephiliac" historiography elaborated by Christian Keathley, who has linked this style's origin with Benjamin and Kracauer. Although Keathley only provided French examples of employing the cinephilia he is after in full force (in "photogenie", *Cahiers du Cinema*, Andre Bazin, etc.), he is, nonetheless, able to use the Germans to conceive of an "irrational history—a historical practice that focuses on discarded or ignored facts of the past."[48] Like the New History, this attention to the overlooked elements parallels the influence photographic media had on society, where spectators came to scan images for any extra object unintentionally caught on film.

As historians of the 1920s lamented the diminishing readership of historiography, others formally responded. Like Stefan Zweig's and Alfred Döblin's historical fiction, which focused on detailing prominent figures, Sergeant published a widely read account of Anne Boleyn in 1924. Taking up the call for new history, he literally "portray[ed] the infatuation of Henry VIII for Anne Boleyn." Sergeant included images and excessively described the attire and appearance of the period. As he worded it, although "the general body of historians still continue[d] ... to shut their eyes to what really matters," Sergeant's historiographical intervention was capturing the specific "character—the soul if you like—beneath the label."[49] His book appearing shortly after the release of Ernst Lubitsch's historical drama *Anna Boleyn* (1920), or *Deception* (1921) in America, bled the two mediums together. He had hoped to open historians' eyes to overlooked features of Anne Boleyn by infusing his writing with the detailed visual elements found in film.

To be sure, eyes were being opened as written forms responded to the swelling audience numbers and box office returns. Even general academic interest in the medium of film was on the rise. As more popular history writing incorporated thick description and psychological detail, rivaling the appeal of film, attempts were also made to analyze and historicize cinema itself. Although there were only eight dissertation topics that dealt directly with film before 1919, from 1919 to 1945 over 200 appeared in Germany alone.[50] The medium was being treated seriously and its popular and academic familiarity was infusing historical thought. It is not that film and visual media had eradicated or completely supplanted historicist historiography, but rather that because of nineteenth-century historicism's, dominance film was able to enjoy a privileged appeal among mass audiences. Were it not for the rise of historicism and its subsequent "crisis," history represented on film would not have garnered such praise (or ridicule), nor affected historical consciousness so powerfully. Because of their relationship, film and history could be coupled to help to train spectators and historians to open their eyes and look in "new" and insightful ways.

Dynamite and Dynamization

Unlike the last few decades of the twentieth century, when the belated reception of Benjamin and Kracauer helped to influence massive shifts in historiography and film studies, Weimar Germany's history writing remained mostly conservative. The general historiography of the Weimar Republic saw only a limited intentional revision.[51] Many historians probably felt as outspoken Lamprecht-critic Georg von Below did in 1920, when he stated that he knew no reason to change the way history was being done despite the talk of a crisis in history writing.[52] And the position of many academic historians clearly indicated a general trend toward conservation. In fact, many university professors pushed back against the surging efforts to reform pedagogical method and spirit following the war. They even supported the Right in rejecting the adoption of the innovative history textbook, *Synoptische Geschichtstabellen.*[53]

Troeltsch also seemed mired in traditionalism. Although Troeltsch had acknowledged and taken up the challenge of ruptured historical thought, he was unable to truly make the relativistic leap "in which we move from the past into the future through our own decision and responsibility."[54] Yet, as perceptive moviegoers and theorists committed to interrogating modernity's problems within the very surfaces of modernity, Benjamin and Kracauer were more willing to take the "tiger's leap" into the past through film. As outsiders to the discipline of history, they approached the crisis of historicism through their radical understanding of photographic media.

Photography and film informed both Benjamin's and Kracauer's notions of historicism and alternative historical methods. Benjamin despised historicism's linking of past to present as inevitable and understood the filmic form as capable of supplying the necessary "dynamite" to explode traditional historiography and ways of seeing the world. The turn to violent imagery and his search for handbooks on "the use and manufacture of nitroglycerine, dynamite bombs [and] poisons," marked Benjamin's growing urgency and frustration, already apparent in his essay, "The Work of Art in the Age of Mechanical Reproducibility."[55] Revolutionary ruminations on the past and history pepper Benjamin's writings. Even some of his ambiguous but revolutionary terms stem from a desire to inform the present with the past. One such debated concept is Benjamin's "optical unconscious."

The optical unconscious stands as the connective tissue between Benjamin's ongoing project of remembering what has been forgotten and Freud's recognition that everything bears meaning in its ties to past experience. The optical unconscious was facilitated by the camera's ability to capture everything put in front of it, even seemingly insignificant details. By revealing the viewer's world anew—reproduced through photography— new insights were made available and the visual "prison world" was burst asunder through "the dynamite of the split second." By adapting cinematic techniques, Benjamin hoped to harness this explosive power of film in his own *writing*. In this regard, Benjamin perfectly enacted the influence of film on historical thought and writing. One medium infused the other.

Benjamin was already experimenting with filmic conventions, like imagery and montage, in his early drafts of the "Artwork" essay. Hansen astutely recognized that essay's filmic structure as sections "arranged to suggest alternating camera setups or, to use Benjamin's words, a 'sequence of positional views.'"[56] This method should help to realize Benjamin's desired outcome in the incomplete *Arcades Project*—"to show, rather than tell"— and approximate the modern power of filmic montage through historiographical juxtaposition. Images or aphoristic statements could be brought into constellation in an effort to reproduce that explosive power of camera vision and montage.

Although multiple camera placements could develop a revealing montage of perspectives, the components were still relative to the camera position and shot frame, or for similarly conceived interdisciplinary history (at the time primarily sociological, constitutional, and economic),[57] their equivalent in the historian's own personal perspective or historical "embeddedness." The cubist-like attempt to shoot the object of study from varying points, as methodological blueprint for Benjamin, was the result of film inflecting historical analysis. Benjamin's thought seemed an intensification of New History while adding much-needed self-consciousness and media theory. For Benjamin, the "fragmentary experience of the modern age" and its technologies could be recuperated "through an unorthodox form of historiography that would itself be fragmentary."[58] The source material for such history writing "flashed up" and required illumination. "The past flits by. The past can be seized only as an image which flashes up at the instant when it can be recognized and is never seen again."[59] In this, Benjamin also filtered his description of the past through film and photographic language—breaking up the flowing past into a series of still frames.

A cinematically understood past required a likewise informed methodology and presentation. By showing rather than telling, Benjamin's historiography bore revolutionary potential as an explosive alarm clock of sorts. The "technique of awakening" Benjamin desired was meant to directly instigate an "awakening from the nineteenth century,"[60] and its twin tyrannies of historicism and capitalism. Benjamin's method was also a deliberately radical opposition to the mounting National Socialist utilization of historiography. Thus, his efforts to wrap historical materialism around a filmic infrastructure lay bare a brilliant and desperate experiment. He could make historical method turn against historicism, as Körner did in *Anders*. Because of this desire, Benjamin's aphoristic description of alternative and cinematic historical method from 1940, in his *Theses on the Concept of History*, remains insightful and provocative, even if opaque.

As the ultimate compilation of his explosive thought, the *Theses* text brings a series of images into collision and offers critiques of Rankean historicism and Marxist materialist historiography in turn.[61] With his biting images bearing the influence of multiple media, Benjamin hoped to enact and inspire an explosion of the continuum of history. Rather than include literal visual images pasted into the written text, Benjamin leaned on the form of writing to approximate the filmic medium. That "dynamite of the split second" in the "Artwork" essay could possibly provide the model necessary to "explode open the continuum of history" proposed in the *Theses*. It is interesting to note that new historian Carl Becker, wrote his "Everyman his own Historian" essay in 1931, espousing a relativistic view of history shaped by "the most diverse threads of information," (including radio, newsreels, films, etc.) and later admitted in a personal letter that the essay's message had some "dynamite" in it.[62] It is Benjamin's text, however, that has exploded through the academy offering ambiguous tools for new types of history. While perhaps not precisely what Benjamin had in mind, his texts' delayed detonation within historicism has revealed some of the potential of film-inspired dynamite.

Kracauer, on the other hand, espoused a modern form of dynamization. He envisioned the media of film and photography as offering perception in new and dynamic ways. There existed a revolutionary potential for photographic media to "make things transparent by simultaneously documenting and decontextualizing."[63] This formal capacity would intersect with Kracauer's thoughts on historiography as well. Kracauer not only approached the subject of history and film earlier (in the mid-1920s) than Benjamin, but was also able to revisit it in his 1960 book, *Theory of Film*, and again in his last and posthumously published work, *History: The Last Things Before the Last*. Equally setting himself apart from Benjamin, Kracauer reveals himself, through his writings, to be an avid filmgoer, who is strikingly familiar with individual films. But he wasn't just taking in films. Kracauer's attention surveyed myriad cultural phenomena with deft analysis. His comments on Troeltsch, in a piece titled "The Crisis of Science,"[64] also attest to his early mental exertion toward the quandary historiography faced.

The 1923 article begins, "[t]he crisis of science–which is by now a topic of commonplace discussion–is most visible in the empirical sciences such as history and sociology." Kracauer's analysis revealed how both Max Weber and Troeltsch attempted to work through the crisis of science and the dilemma of historicism or relativity, but with no lasting success. Kracauer argued, "In contrast to Weber, Troeltsch is right to link the construction of contexts of meaning to valuations. Contrary to what he believes, however, within the framework of scientific discovery such valuations may not be allowed to cross the line from the relative into the absolute."[65] The relativity of standpoints, value decisions, and temporal perspectives are analogous with Benjamin's camera setups—each producing important insights, while shaping the construction of the same. But Kracauer was on to something.

Deep in thought about film and photography, Kracauer proceeded to develop an intermedial style of historical thought. His deliberate working through history with filmic inflection in his 1927 "Photography" essay then responded to Troeltsch's call for historiography from "confident and courageous men ... not skeptics or mystics, not rationalistic fanatics and not omniscient historians." Kracauer's film-inspired mode—while unabashedly relative and subjective—shed light on otherwise neglected elements of modernity. He could notice the unnoticed and capture it like film/photography, by documenting and de-(re)contextualing. This step was significant since it marked an exploration outside the strict mode of historicist thought.

Kracauer's intervention remains instructive, since for over a century historicism has come to permeate "our very mode of cognition, our way or ordering and explaining the past," and thinking outside this mode has been difficult for historians. The cultural regimes of historicity, in the plural, that govern what is felt, understood, and even retained of the past have been deeply shaped by the historicist approach. Yet, what Kracauer seems to have realized is that film could affect an important shift in this regard and shape a cinematic regime of sensing what is past and what is "historical," even our sense of temporality. Progressive thinkers like Kracauer, correlated photographic media with historicism and considered their effect on cognition.

His couching of historiography or historical theory in filmic language alone was telling. Koch reminds us that "Kracauer emphasizes that a not inconsiderable part of the meaning generated by history depends on the language in which historiography is written and history portrayed. The historian resorts to 'formal expedients involving structure and composition.'"[66] The surfacing metalanguage for historiography in filmic figurations bore a distinct significance. Beyond shifts in language and metaphors for the past cinema could change the experience of history and some of this sensation could possibly translate into the written word.

Kracauer consciously considered the experience of history for sensorially altered bodies. If film was shaping a different audience for historical representation, then historicism would need an overhaul. This provided methodological challenges. Kracauer candidly wrote in a letter to Erwin Panofsky of his intent to "blend the 'historical approach' with the 'phenomenological' one."[67] Hansen described Kracauer's adaptation of Husserl's *Lebenswelt* as a means of dealing with the "methodological problems of historiography with recourse to the 'photographic approach.'"[68] In an effort to combine historiography and photography, or to rethink historiography through photographic media, Kracauer produced some of the most provocative thoughts, even if he didn't always follow them through. One such thought was the corporeal experience of film and, by extension, history on film.

Kracauer recognized that truly cinematic films engaged the material reality of the human body of the viewer. Because of this, Kracauer has been seen to forward an "ethics of enjoyment" and a "sensualist theory of filmic perception."[69] But Kracauer was at pains to reconcile his sensory understanding of film reception with the medium's effect on history and memory[70]. The primary objection to some historical films for Kracauer then was that historical content was not portrayed in a narrative structure appropriate to the time. Modernity required dynamized historical representation.

Thus, Kracauer's problem with *Film d'art* in the "Marseille Notebooks" is that the genre, emblemized by the historical film *The Assassination of the Duke de Guise* (1908), "functions as a metaphor for a historically obsolete, static, and anthropocentric regime of perception and experience."[71] The *Film d'art* continues static theatrical staging instead of "dynamizing perception" through camera angle, cycling between varied proximities to the subject, and conspicuous editing. It is not historical or literary content, but the form of presentation that should correlate with, while shaping, a modern sensorium. And the modern sensorium was responding to technology, shocks, and urban mass culture.

In this important respect, the death of Troeltsch also coincided with the birth of the "unchained camera" and increasingly dynamized, sensuous, and subjective history on screen. With this liberating technological innovation, the camera "cease[d] to be a static spectator registering whatever happens to come in front of it."[72] As Kracauer enthusiastically noted of the camera's use in *The Last Laugh* (1924), "it pans, travels and tilts up and down with a perseverance which not only results in a pictorial narrative of complete fluidity, but also enables the spectator to follow the course of events from various viewpoints."[73] The movement of the liberated "unchained camera" came as a stark contrast to the front shot tableau-style cinematography of most films.

The beginnings of mobilizing the camera in representing the past also appeared in Lubitsch's work. While deriding the films' nihilism, Kracauer commented on how "observers admired the free use of the camera in these Lubitsch pageants." Especially in *Anna Boleyn* (1920), Lubitsch's innovative (pre-unchained) camera movements reflected the new sensorial maturation. Kracauer continued, "[w]hile traditional aesthetics would have condemned such photographs as incoherent, the war generation which had become accustomed to them began enjoying their singular power of expression."[74] Shifts in historical thought and representation equally reflected a new postwar generation of consumers, consumers of images. In cinematography, Lubitsch was heading in the right direction, formally updating history.

Kracauer recognized the revolutionary ability of film to formally subvert historicism. He described historicism as seeking after the photography of time. In the desire to produce a comprehensive "mirroring of a temporal sequence," historicism attempts to provide the "meaning of all that occurred within that time." The aporia of the historicist ideal was being staged by the technological construction of films. Since "the equivalent of [historicism's] temporal photography would be a giant film depicting the temporally interconnected events from every vantage point," the impossibility of the task is made abundantly clear.[75]

The fact that history films provided a comprehensive visual and spatial continuum of display from a single (even if shifting) vantage point made the problematic of the crisis of historicism apparent. No matter how many shots, angles, or even parallel storylines were included, no film could appease the demands of historicism, thereby emphasizing the futility of such attempts. In other words, the deeply theoretical basis of the crisis was made visual and inscribed on the very form of film in general and historical films in a double sense.

Even before Kracauer, Nietzsche had lamented the selective style nineteenth-century historicism had already begun to shape. By perverting the natural relationship of recording the past as "self-production," in favor of an "objective uncovering of facts by the disinterested scholar," historicism constructed a specific type of continuity.[76] As if complete and true, selection was the appearance of objectivity. Unlike invented fictional stories, although they both share narrative structures referring to temporality,[77] histories actually claim to represent humanity to itself, they claim to refer to "actual" events, people, objects, times, and relationships. This aspect, considered by Kracauer to be historicism's "privileged access to the concrete," was also the deciding factor for Paul Ricoeur. Although both are "figurations of temporality," the difference between fictional narratives and historiography for Ricoeur lies in the latter's role as a true allegory of temporality.[78] While most silent films of the period bore such a subjectively viewed display of narrative, the history films married this narratological convention with historical content.

Even though filmed history might offer concrete details, it was not the same as written history. Kracauer's ambivalence toward the medium was captured in his oft-cited wording, where he named the dilemma the "go-for-broke game of history." Despite the argument's lack of full coherence and completion, its timely provocation leapfrogged Troeltsch's project by adding media theory. Kracauer worried that photographic media resulted in an "assault of images" and that "this mass of images is so powerful that it threatens to destroy the potentially existing awareness of crucial traits."[79] Even though mere documentation had no inherent significance there was also a revolutionary potential available in this effect. By exposing what had become second nature, the material building blocks of life represented through film appeared appropriately plastic and their possibility of diverse arrangements reflected the openness of alternatives to the political, social, and economic status quo.

In this regard, Kracauer's last two books can be seen to merge. His theory of film as redeeming reality and his final thoughts on historiography still marry the medium with the craft's possible thought processes. Hansen has brought the two works into productive correlation through closely reading the early "Marseille notebooks" for the thought behind *History*. She highlights the fact that Kracauer consistently thought of photographic media as "capable of advancing and registering disintegration in a material, sensorily graspable form, or archiving the disintegrated particles, and of reconfiguring them toward a different, as yet unknowable order."[80] This role of film in documenting and offering new possibilities could possibly be carried over to a thoroughly modern historiography, with equally revolutionary potential.

In its "privileged access to the concrete" and as an exposé of historicism's problematic nature, film also bore a *revelatory* potential. If photographic media represented the false hope of authority, objectivity, and meaning associated with historicism, its value for Kracauer seemed to lay in exposing these very elements as capable of different configurations. In other words, film and photography bore and staged the crisis of historicism, perhaps better than any other form. If this is true and Kracauer couldn't quite commit to a radical filmic mode of historiography because of the threat that meaning and crucial distinctions would be the casualties, then just what hope did he have in a "photographic approach" to history?

Photographic History

A photographic approach to film, as to history, lies not in objectivity or mere aesthetic construction, but in a specific type of thought and representation—those that foster revelation. For Kracauer, photographic media can galvanize an innovative understanding of the historian's craft. Photography, as the building blocks of film, emphasizes the "fortuitous," the unexpected, and Kracauer held that "random events are the very meat of snapshots." Both "the photographic approach and scientific investigation" analogously "probe into an exhaustive universe whose entirety forever eludes them."[81] The directive to "transmit raw material without defining it" could even describe mash-up histories, like Benjamin's own *Arcades Project*. More than the montage effect desired by Benjamin, Kracauer seems to borrow from photography and film their ability to bring any and everything into the frame.

Photographic media's absolute "inclusion" was a defining aspect that captivated Kracauer. In objectively reproducing everything, both significant and seemingly insignificant, in a variety of angles and distances these media problematized traditional nineteenth-century-style historiography. Like the New History's expanded panoramic gaze or stylistic experiments, and also like the cinematic examples of historical vision in individual films, "photographic history" could provide new *histories* rather than a hermetic *History*. Kracauer's later explanations of the pitfalls of traditional historicism reveal the figural potential of film. Nineteenth-century historicism was too linear and closed, too broad and general. Historians needed to move from the long shot approach to close-ups and dynamic cutting between.

Kracauer wrote to Adorno in 1949 describing their "age in which scientific interest in the links between the smallest elements is increasingly surpassing the dynamism of major ideas." Kracauer then made the conscious choice to "couch it in the language of film" and explained that "the aesthetics of film can be assigned to an epoch in which the 'long-shot' perspective, which believed that in some way focused on the absolute, is replaced by a 'close-up' perspective, which instead sheds light on the meaning of individuated things, of the fragment."[82] He draped the "aesthetics of film" over intellectual investigation. The result: the dynamism then shifts from the content of "major ideas" themselves over into the form of investigating the "smallest elements" and shooting in "close-up."

Not surprisingly, the core principles of the late-twentieth century trend in microhistory were said by Carlo Ginzburg to have been summed up in Kracauer's description of the shift from long shot to close-up. Ginzburg related, that the "posthumous pages of Kracauer's, a nonprofessional historian, still constitute today ... the best introduction to microhistory."[83] Similar connections could be made with aspects of the cultural poetics of "new historicism."

Drawing on Wolfgang Schivelbusch's study of railway-conditioned perception, Keathley has noted how the movement of new historicism also exhibits a searching, panoramic, and even film-inspired gaze. This gaze, translated into historiography, might more broadly be the result of new forms of seeing—a modern cultural shift toward gazing. Usually beginning with the anecdotal, new historicism shifts between close-ups and focuses attention toward literary or historical detritus. These elements and texts are often not only seemingly disconnected but also insignificant, or in Kracauer's words "seemingly unimportant details."[84] Much like the scenes of historical projection in films mentioned earlier, new historicism often uncovers forgotten or unimagined peoples, texts, and connections. The result of new historicism, as well as microhistory, is often a sense of intimacy with (even incredibly foreign) historical subjects and sources, who have been plucked out of the murky flow of the past. As if taking a magnifying glass to the edges of an old photograph, these neglected elements can be rendered anew in close-up.

Micro and "new histories" also offered a novel approach to the problem of proximity in historiography. They shifted the use of the frame in history by focusing on notation and discourse rather than presenting the past as a milestone to our present. Treating the general and the particular has ever been a problem for historicism. In "The Role of the Particular and the General in the Study of Universal History" Ranke himself stated, "[r]elating the particular to the general cannot harm research. Without a general view, research would become sterile; without exact research, the general view would deteriorate into fantasy."[85] Traditional history was often too distant and critical to have significance or offer meaningful experience. These more recent historiographical trends or "new historicisms" latched on to Kracauer's recognition that photographic media can register both particular details as well as engender emotional connections, offering both cold distance and a certain closeness, as an index and record of time and space. For similar reasons, both newer historicisms and historical films have been criticized for being simultaneously too much and not enough.

As the past became more cinematic in modern thought, its analysis more closely aligned with slowing the flow of life (as the past) to a still frame and scanning for flashes from the past. Some historians came to hope for, look for, even expect unprecedented inspiration from the historical sources themselves.[86] These sources—scraps, scribblings, events, and mentalities—should flash-up and reveal themselves in the unexplored margins, offering new connections and connotations. After the crisis of historicism and the saturation of society in film and images, the past became, like photographic media, a surface that required more to unlock than mere critical distance. There has developed an increased need for a certain historiographical proximity, one that could work like film by being close enough for experience and revelation and distant enough for narration, sharing (making collective), and criticism.

Historiography and "historicisms" of the last few decades have taken on elements of film, not just because of the proliferation of audiovisual media,[87] but also because of our own reception in the late twentieth century of these Weimar thinkers and a potential that rested latent until we finally began to comprehend its force. Perhaps the photographic media since the Second World War had influenced historians enough that by the 1990s we were finally ready to implement the kinds of cinematic views of the past described by Benjamin and Kracauer decades earlier. It would appear then, that through the influence of media and its attendant experiences and insights, some strands of historiography had caught up with Weimar historical thought. Like the revelatory and often overlooked items in a photograph or film, Benjamin and Kracauer—at the margins of the Frankfurt school and historical discipline—continue to reward historians willing to look and grasp their flashes of inspiration.

Recognizing the pivotal role, photographic media played in both Kracauer's and Benjamin's rethinking of history in crisis helps to unlock the potential of cinematic ways of feeling and conceiving of history. Their insights can also help wrest Weimar history films from their teleological link with Nazi pageantry. This mindset, then, seems entirely appropriate for concluding this study. To detonate the potential of early Weimar's cinematic relationship to the past and temporality one must employ an augmented historicism. The film-inspired detonation of accepted chronology brings an alternative history, even redemptive history, of early Weimar—evinced through its relationship to historical film—into relief. It might also force Weimar's entanglement of cinema, history, and embodiment into productive collision with our own.

Notes

1 Franklin H. Giddings, "A Theory of History," *Political Science Quarterly* 35, no. 4 (December 1, 1920): 496.
2 See Mark D. Chapman, "The 'Sad Story' of Ernst Troeltsch's Proposed British Lectures of 1923," *Zeitschrift Für Neuere Theologiegeschichte (Journal for the History of Modern Theology)* 1, no. 1 (January 1994): 97–122.
3 Wilhelm Pauck, *Harnack and Troeltsch: Two Historical Theologians*, Drew University. Drew Lectureship in Biography 1967 (New York, NY: Oxford University Press, 1968), 124.
4 Georg G. Iggers, *Deutsche Geschichtswissenschaft: eine Kritik der traditionellen Geschichtsauffassung von Herder bis zur Gegenwart* (Vienna: Böhlau Verlag, 1997), 164.
5 Pauck, *Harnack and Troeltsch*, 124.
6 Reinhart Koselleck, *Futures Past: On the Semantics of Historical Time*, trans. Keith Tribe (New York, NY: Columbia University Press, 1985), 42, 258.
7 Charles R. Bambach, *Heidegger, Dilthey, and the Crisis of Historicism* (Ithaca, NY: Cornell University Press, 1995), 41.
8 Gustav Würtenberg, "Geschichtsunterricht und Kino," *Vergangenheit und Gegenwart* 18, no. 6 (1928): 361.
9 Eduardo Cadava, *Words of Light: Theses on the Photography of History* (Princeton, NJ: Princeton University Press, 1997), xxi.
10 Friedrich Schiller, "What Is Universal History and to What End Does One Study It," in *German Essays on History: Hegel, Ranke, Spengler, and Others*, 1st ed., ed. Rolf Sältzer (London: Bloomsbury Academic, 1991), 30.
11 Nicholas Baer, "Metaphysics of Finitude: *Der müde Tod* and the Crisis of Historicism," in *A Companion to Fritz Lang*, 1st ed., ed. Joe McElhaney (Malden, MA: Wiley-Blackwell, 2015), 142.
12 Hayden White, "Historiography and Historiophoty," *The American Historical Review* 93, no. 5 (December 1, 1988): 1193.
13 Miriam Hansen, *Babel and Babylon: Spectatorship in American Silent Film* (Cambridge, MA: Harvard University Press, 1991), 137.
14 Richard Oswald, "Die Aussichten des Grossen Historischen Films auf dem Weltmarkt," *Der Kinematograph* 806 (1922), 60.
15 Ranke discussed this relationship in his "Autobiographical Dictation" of November 1885. See Leopold von Ranke, *The Secret of World History: Selected Writings on the Art and Science of History*, ed. Roger Wines (Bronx, NY: Fordham University Press, 1981), 33.
16 Sylvia Paletschek, *Popular Historiographies in the 19th and 20th Centuries: Cultural Meanings, Social Practices* (New York, NY: Berghahn Books, 2011), 39.
17 Hayden White shows the novelistic and generic conventions of the nineteenth century that shaped historiography in his *Metahistory* (Baltimore, MD: Johns

Hopkins University Press, 1975). See also Kathrin Maurer, *Discursive Interaction: Literary Realism and Academic Historiography in Nineteenth-Century Germany* (Heidelberg: Synchron, 2006).

18 Herbert Ihering, "Das Weib des Pharao," *Berliner Börsen-Courier*, March 15, 1922, Evening Edition reproduced in *Lubitsch*, eds. Hans Helmut Prinzler and Enno Patalas (Munich: Bucher, 1984), 99.

19 Schiller uses the figure of the world stage, see Schiller, *German Essays on History*, 33. In a similar manner, Kant uses the motif in his introduction to "Idea for a Universal History from a Cosmopolitan Point of View."

20 For Walter Benjamin, the past flits by as images in his "Theses on the Philosophy of History," in *Illuminations* (New York, NY: Houghton Mifflin Harcourt, 1968), 255.

21 Alexander Demandt, *Metaphern für Geschichte: Sprachbilder und Gleichnisse im historisch-politischen Denken* (Munich: Beck, 1978), 348.

22 W. J. T. Mitchell and Mark B. N. Hansen, *Critical Terms for Media Studies* (Chicago, IL: University of Chicago Press, 2010), 41.

23 For example, Descartes understood the eye through workings of the camera obscura. Douwe Draaisma, *Metaphors of Memory: A History of Ideas about the Mind* (Cambridge, MA: Cambridge University Press, 2000), 105–6. Freud used film, trains, and writing pads to conceptualize the mind and memory. Thomas Elsaesser, "Freud as Media Theorist: Mystic Writing Pads and the Matter of Memory," *Screen* 50 (2009): 100–13.

24 Mitchell and Hansen, *Critical Terms*, 40–41.

25 Siegfried Kracauer, *The Mass Ornament: Weimar Essays* (Cambridge, MA: Harvard University Press, 1995), 50.

26 Giddings, "A Theory of History," 496–99.

27 Joseph Zsuffa, *Béla Balázs: The Man and the Artist* (Oakland, CA: University of California Press, 1987), 57.

28 James Joyce's correspondences quoted in John McCourt, *Roll Away the Reel World: James Joyce and Cinema* (Ireland: Cork University Press, 2010), 9.

29 Sabine Hake, *German National Cinema* (London: Routledge, 2008), 40.

30 Alfred Döblin, "Ulysses by Joyce," *The Weimar Republic Sourcebook*, eds. Anton Kaes, Martin Jay, and Edward Dimendberg (repr., Oakland, CA: University of California Press, 1995), 514.

31 Vivian Sobchack, "The Insistent Fringe: Moving Images and Historical Consciousness," *History and Theory* 36, no. 4 (December 1, 1997): 5.

32 Stuart Macintyre, Juan Maiguashca, and Attila Pók, *The Oxford History of Historical Writing: Volume 4: 1800–1945* (Oxford: Oxford University Press, 2011), 177.

33 Michael Whelan, "James Harvey Robinson, the New History, and the 1916 Social Studies Report," *The History Teacher* 24, no. 2 (February 1, 1991): 193.

34 James Harvey Robinson, *The New History: Essays Illustrating the Modern Historical Outlook* (London: The Macmillan Company, 1912), 24.

35 James Harvey Robinson, *The Mind in the Making* (New York, NY: Harper, 1921), 5.

36 Whelan, "James Harvey Robinson," 195.

37 Quoted in Pfitzer, *Popular History and the Literary Marketplace, 1840–1920* (Amherst: University of Massachusetts Press, 2008), 183.

38 D. C. Knowlton, "The New History and the Photoplay," *Historical Outlook* 19, no. 2 (February 1, 1928): 70.

39 Ibid., 73.

40 Carl Becker, "Mr. Wells and the New History," *The American Historical Review* 26, no. 4 (July 1, 1921): 642.

41 "History as Popular Reading," *New York Times*, August 9, 1925, 16.

42 "Rewriting History," *New York Times*, September 12, 1921, 9.

43 Ernst Troeltsch, "Angelsächsische Ansicht der Weltgeschichte," *Historische Zeitschrift*, B. 126, H. 2 (1922): 278–79.

44 Becker, "Mr. Wells and the New History," 643.

45 "Professors Assail History by Wells," *New York Times*, May 9, 1922, 13.

46 *New York Times*, November 14, 1920, 25.

47 Robinson, *The New History*, 136.

48 See Christian Keathley, *Cinephilia and History, or The Wind in the Trees* (Bloomington, IL: Indiana University Press, 2006), 130.

49 Philip W. Sergeant, *The Life of Anne Boleyn* (Whitefish, MT: Kessinger Publishing, 2005), v.

50 Paolo Cherchi Usai, Lorenzo Codelli, and Jan-Christopher Horak, *Prima di Caligari: cinema tedesco, 1895–1920* (Pordenone: Edizioni Biblioteca dell'immagine, 1990), 360.

51 Hans Schleier, *Die Bürgerliche Deutsche Geschichtsschreibung Der Weimarer Republik*, Schriften Des Zentralinstituts Für Geschichte 40 (Berlin: Akademie-Verlag, 1975), 22.

52 Georg von Below, *Die parteiamtliche neue Geschichtsaffassung. Ein Beitrag zur Frage der historischen Objektivität* (Langensalza, 1920), 53–54, quoted in Hans Schleier, *Die bürgerliche deutsche Geschichtsschreibung der Weimarer Republik* (Berlin: Akademie-Verlag, 1975), 23.

53 Frederick William Roman, *The New Education in Europe: An Account of Recent Fundamental Changes in the Educational Philosophy of Great Britain, France and Germany*, 2 ed. (London: New York: G. Routledge; E. P. Dutton, 1924), 197.

54 Kracauer, *The Mass Ornament*, 216.

55 Esther Leslie, *Walter Benjamin* (London: Reaktion Books, 2007), 172.

56 Miriam Bratu Hansen, *Cinema and Experience: Siegfried Kracauer, Walter Benjamin, and Theodor W. Adorno* (Oakland, CA: University of California Press, 2011), 88.

57 Karl Lamprecht and Otto Hintze were examples of "anti-historist" historians who sought to imbue the craft with methodological borrowings from other fields. See Macintyre, Maiguashca, and Pók, *The Oxford History*, 176.

58 Rashna Wadia Richards, *Cinematic Flashes: Cinephilia and Classical Hollywood* (Bloomington, IL: Indiana University Press, 2012), 4.

59 Benjamin, *Illuminations*, 255.

60 Quoted in Vanessa R. Schwartz, "Walter Benjamin for Historians," *The American Historical Review* 106, no. 5 (December 1, 2001): 1728.

61 Phillipe Simay, "Tradition as Injunction: Benjamin and the Critique of Historicisms," in *Walter Benjamin and History*, ed. Andrew E. Benjamin (London: Continuum International Publishing Group, 2005), 137.

62 Milton M. Klein, "Everyman His Own Historian: Carl Becker as Historiographer," *The History Teacher* 19, no. 1 (November 1, 1985): 106.

63 John R. Hall, Blake Stimson, and Lisa Tamiris Becker, *Visual Worlds* (New York: Routledge, 2005), 154.

64 Kracauer, *The Mass Ornament*, 213–223.

65 Ibid., 222.

66 Gertrud Koch, *Siegfried Kracauer: An Introduction* (Princeton, NJ: Princeton University Press, 2000), 118.

67 Letter to Panofsky, 6 November, 1949, in *Siegfried Kracauer—Erwin Panofsky Briefwechsel, 1941–1966*, ed. Volker Breidecker (Berlin: Akademie Verlag, 1996), 55.

68 Hansen, *Cinema and Experience*, 272.

69 Koch, *Siegfried Kracauer*, 103.

70 See Chapter 1.

71 Hansen, *Cinema and Experience*, 264.

72 Stephen Brockmann, *A Critical History of German Film* (Rochester, NY: Camden House, 2010), 72.

73 Siegfried Kracauer, *From Caligari to Hitler: A Psychological History of the German Film* (Princeton, NJ: Princeton University Press, 1947), 105.

74 Ibid., 53.

75 Kracauer, *The Mass Ornament*, 49–50.

76 Friedrich Wilhelm Nietzsche, *On the Advantage and Disadvantage of History for Life* (Indianapolis, IN: Hackett Publishing, 1980), 2.

77 Hayden V. White, *The Content of the Form: Narrative Discourse and Historical Representation* (Baltimore, MD: John Hopkins University Press, 1987), 176.

78 Ibid., 181.

79 Kracauer, *The Mass Ornament*, 58.

80 Hansen, *Cinema and Experience*, 255–56.

81 Siegfried Kracauer, *Theory of Film: The Redemption of Physical Reality* (Princeton, NJ: Princeton University Press, 1960), 20.

82 Koch, *Siegfried Kracauer*, 96.

83 Carlo Ginzburg, John Tedeschi, and Anne C. Tedeschi, "Microhistory: Two or Three Things That I Know about It," *Critical Inquiry* 20, no. 1 (October 1, 1993): 27.

84 Gerd Gemünden and Johannes von Moltke, *Culture in the Anteroom: The Legacies of Siegfried Kracauer* (Ann Arbor, MI: University of Michigan Press, 2012), 1.

85 Leopold von Ranke, *The Theory and Practice of History: Edited with an Introduction by Georg G. Iggers* (New York: Routledge, 2010), 25.

86 One might recall here Stephen Greenblatt's admission of a desire to "speak with the dead" in *Shakespearean Negotiations: The Circulation of Social Energy in Renaissance England* (Oakland, CA: University of California Press, 1988), 1.

87 Pierre Sorlin, "How to Look at an 'Historical' Film," in *The Historical Film: History and Memory in Media*, ed. Marcia Landy (London: Continuum International Publishing Group, 2001), 25.

Bibliography

"100 Reels of History," *Film Daily* no. 20 (January 1922), 2.

Abel, Richard. *Silent Film*. London: Continuum International Publishing Group, 1996.

Ackerknecht, Erwin. *Das Lichtspiel im Dienste der Bildungspflege: Handbuch für Lichtspielreformer*. Berlin: Weidmann, 1918.

Adorno, Theodor W., and Henry W. Pickford. *Critical Models: Interventions and Catchwords*. New York: Columbia University Press, 2005.

Agamben, Giorgio. *Infancy and History: The Destruction of Experience*. Translated by Liz Heron. London: Verso, 1993.

Altenloh, Emilie. "A Sociology of the Cinema: The Audience." *Screen* 42, no. 3 (September 21, 2001): 249–93.

Anderson, Joseph. *The Reality of Illusion: An Ecological Approach to Cognitive Film Theory*. Carbondale, IL: SIU Press, 1998.

Ankersmit, F. R. *History and Tropology: The Rise and Fall of Metaphor*. Oakland, CA: University of California Press, 1994.

———. *Sublime Historical Experience*. Redwood City, CA: Stanford University Press, 2005.

Arasse, Daniel. *The Guillotine and the Terror*. London: Lane, 1989.

"Auge und Film," *Der Kinematograph*, 756, 1921

Baer, Nicholas. "Metaphysics of Finitude: *Der müde Tod* and the Crisis of Historicism," In *A Companion to Fritz Lang*, 1st ed., edited by Joe McElhaney, 141–60. Malden, MA: Wiley-Blackwell, 2015.

Balázs, Béla. *Der Sichtbare Mensch Oder Die Kultur Des Films*, 4th ed. Berlin: Suhrkamp Verlag, 2001.

Bambach, Charles R. *Heidegger, Dilthey, and the Crisis of Historicism*. Ithaca, NY: Cornell University Press, 1995.

Barker, Jennifer M. *The Tactile Eye: Touch and the Cinematic Experience*. Oakland, CA: University of California Press, 2009.

Becker, Carl. "Mr. Wells and the New History." *The American Historical Review* 26, no. 4 (July 1921): 641–56.

Benjamin, Andrew E. *Walter Benjamin and History*. London: Continuum International Publishing Group, 2005.

Benjamin, Walter. *The Arcades Project*. Cambridge, MA: Harvard University Press, 1999.

Benjamin, Walter, Howard Eiland, and Michael W. Jennings. *Walter Benjamin: Selected Writings, Volume 3: 1935–1938*. Vol. 3. Cambridge, MA: Harvard University Press, 2002.

Benjamin, Walter, Michael William Jennings, and Rodney Livingstone. *Walter Benjamin*. Cambridge, MA: Harvard University Press, 2005.

Benkwitz, Gustav. "Geschichtsstudium und Film," *Der Kinematograph* 756, 1921.

Beyfuss, E. (Edgar), and A. Kossowsky. *Das Kulturfilmbuch/Unter Mitwirkung Namhafter Fachleute Herausgegeben von E. Beyfuss Und A. Kossowsky*. Berlin: Carl P. Chryselius, 1924.

Boese, Carl. *Der Film* 15, April 12, 1919.

Boym, Svetlana. *The Future of Nostalgia*. New York: Basic Books, 2001.

Brockmann, Stephen. *A Critical History of German Film*. Rochester, NY: Camden House, 2010.

"Brought into Focus," *New York Times*, January 30, 1921, X2

"Brought into Focus," *New York Times*, April 24, 1921, X2.

Buckland, Warren. *The Cognitive Semiotics of Film*. Cambridge: New York: Cambridge University Press, 2000.

Bukatman, Scott. "Vivian Sobchack in Conversation with Scott Bukatman," *E-media Studies* 2, no. 1 (2009).

Burgoyne, Robert. *The Epic Film*. New York: Taylor & Francis, 2011.

Cadava, Eduardo. *Words of Light: Theses on the Photography of History*. Princeton, NJ: Princeton University Press, 1997.

Carringer, Robert L. *Ernst Lubitsch: A Guide to References and Resources. A Reference Publication in Film*. Boston: G. K. Hall, 1978.

Carr, Nicholas. "Is Google Making Us Stupid?: What the Internet Is Doing to Our Brains." *The Atlantic* 302, no. 1 (2008): 56–63.

Carr, Nicholas. *The Shallows: What the Internet Is Doing to Our Brains*. New York: W. W. Norton & Company, 2011.

Chapman, Mark D. "The 'sad Story' of Ernst Troeltsch's Proposed British Lectures of 1923." *Zeitschrift Für Neuere Theologiegeschichte [Journal for the History of Modern Theology]* 1, no. 1 (January 1994): 97–122.

Cohen, Sol. "An Innocent Eye: The 'Pictorial Turn,' Film Studies, and History." *History of Education Quarterly* 43, no. 2 (July 1, 2003): 250–61.

Coudenhove-Kalergi, Richard Nicolaus. *Pan-Europa*. 1.–5. tausend. Wien: Pan-Europa-verlag, 1923.

Curthoys, Ann, and Marylin Lake. *Connected Worlds: History in Transnational Perspective*. Canberra: Australian National University E Press, 2005.

Debord, Guy, and Ken Knabb. *Society of the Spectacle*. Black & Red, 2006.

Deleuze, Gilles. *Cinema: The Time-Image*. Minneapolis, MN: University of Minnesota Press, 1989.

Demandt, Alexander. *Metaphern für Geschichte: Sprachbilder und Gleichnisse im historisch-politischen Denken*. Beck, 1978.

"Der Deutsche Spielfilm und das Ausland," *Der Kinematograph* 780.

114   *Bibliography*

"Der Falsche Fitz: Friederich II im Film," in *Potsdam Filmmuseum*, 2012 exhibit.
"Der Lehrfilm in den Preussischen Schulen," *Deutsche Lichtspiel-Zeitung* n. 18, 1920, 4.
"Die Lubitsch-Filmstadt," *Der Kinematograph* 15 (December 1921): 774.
"Discusses Movies as an Aid to Culture." *New York Times*, July 30, 1924, 4.
Dilthey, Wilhelm, Rudolf A. Makkreel, and Frithjof Rodi. *Hermeneutics and the Study of History*. Princeton, NJ: Princeton University Press, 1996.
Doane, Mary Ann. *The Emergence of Cinematic Time: Modernity, Contingency, the Archive*. Cambridge, MA: Harvard University Press, 2002.
Draaisma, Douwe. *Metaphors of Memory: A History of Ideas about the Mind*. Cambridge, UK: Cambridge University Press, 2000.
"Eine Völkerbundtat der Filmindstrie," *Film-Kurier*, August 4, 1920.
Eisner, Lotte H. *The Haunted Screen: Expressionism in the German Cinema and the Influence of Max Reinhardt*. Oakland, CA: University of California Press, 1969.
Eller, Paul. "Geschichtsstudium und Film," *Der Kinematograph* 752, (1921).
Eller, Paul. "Geschichtsstudium und Film: Eine Entgegnung," *Der Kinematograph* 758 (1921).
Elsaesser, Thomas. "Freud as Media Theorist: Mystic Writing Pads and the Matter of Memory," *Screen* 50 (2009): 100–13.
Elsaesser, Thomas. *Weimar Cinema and After: Germany's Historical Imaginary*. New York: Routledge, 2000.
Elsaesser, Thomas, and Michael Wedel. *A Second Life: German Cinema's First Decades*. Amsterdam: Amsterdam University Press, 1996.
Engeler, Knut. *Geschichtsunterricht und Reformpädagogik*. Germany: LIT Verlag Münster, 2009.
Eyman, Scott. *Ernst Lubitsch: Laughter in Paradise*. Baltimore, MD: JHU Press, 2000.
Fairbanks, Douglas. "Let Me Say This for the Films," in Wyeth, *The Ladies' Home Journal* (September 1922), 120.
"Filmreisen und Lehrfilm," *Der Kinematograph*, 776, 1922.
Fischer, Kuno. *Geschichte der neuern philosophie: Bd. Kant's System der reinen Vernunft auf Grund der Vernunftkritik. 1869*. Heidelberg: F. Bassermann, 1869.
Friedell, Egon. "Dubarry," *Weltbühne* 17 (March 10, 1921), 276.
Friedfeld, Joseph. "Jenseits der Grenze," *Weltbühne* 27 (July 6, 1922), 4.
Fuhrmann, Wolfgang. *Imperial Projections: Screening the German Colonies*. New York: Berghahn, 2015.
Gadamer, Hans-Georg. *Truth and Method*. London: Continuum International Publishing Group, 2004.
Ganeva, Mila. *Women in Weimar Fashion: Discourses & Displays in German Culture, 1918–1933*. Reprint. Rochester, NY: Camden House, 2008.
Gemunden, Gerd, and Johannes von Moltke. *Culture in the Anteroom: The Legacies of Siegfried Kracauer*. Ann Arbor, MI: University of Michigan Press, 2012.
Gess, Nicola. "Gaining Sovereignty: On the Figure of the Child in Walter Benjamin's Writing," *MLN* 125, no. 3 (2010): 682–708.
Giddings, Franklin H. "A Theory of History." *Political Science Quarterly* 35, no. 4 (December 1, 1920): 493–521.

Ginzburg, Carlo, John Tedeschi, and Anne C. Tedeschi. "Microhistory: Two or Three Things That I Know about It." *Critical Inquiry* 20, no. 1 (October 1, 1993): 10–35.

Görs, Britta, Nikolaos Psarros, and Paul Ziche. *Wilhelm Ostwald at the Crossroads Between Chemistry, Philosophy and Media Culture.* Leipzig: Leipziger Universitätsverlag, 2005.

Greenblatt, Stephen Jay, and Stephen Greenblatt. *Shakespearean Negotiations: The Circulation of Social Energy in Renaissance England.* Oakland: University of California Press, 1988.

Griffith, David Wark. *The Rise and Fall of Free Speech in America,* [no publisher] 1916.

Groot, Jerome de. *Consuming History: Historians and Heritage in Contemporary Popular Culture.* London: Routledge, 2009.

Hake, Sabine. *German National Cinema.* London: Routledge, 2008.

———. *Passions and Deceptions: The Early Films of Ernst Lubitsch.* Princeton, NJ: Princeton University Press, 1992.

———. *The Cinema's Third Machine: Writing on Film in Germany, 1907–1933.* Lincoln, NE: University of Nebraska Press, 1993.

Hall, John R., Blake Stimson, and Lisa Tamiris Becker. *Visual Worlds.* New York: Taylor & Francis, 2005.

Hanke, Barbara. *Geschichtskultur an höheren Schulen von der Wilhelminischen Ära bis zum Zweiten Weltkrieg: Das Beispiel Westfalen.* Germany: LIT Verlag Münster, 2011.

Hansen, Mark B. N. *New Philosophy for New Media.* Cambridge, MA: MIT Press, 2004.

Hansen, Miriam. "The Mass Production of the Senses: Classical Cinema as Vernacular Modernism." *Modernism/modernity* 6, no. 2 (1999): 59–77.

———. *Cinema and Experience: Siegfried Kracauer, Walter Benjamin, and Theodor W. Adorno.* Oakland, CA: University of California Press, 2011.

———. *Babel and Babylon: Spectatorship in American Silent Film.* Cambridge, MA: Harvard University Press, 1991.

Hartog, François. "Time and Heritage." *Museum International* 57, no. 3 (2005): 7–18.

Herder, Johann Gottfried. *Outlines of a Philosophy of the History of Man: Johann Gottfried Von Herder. Tr. from the German of John Godfrey Herder by T. Churchill.* Luke Hansard, 1803.

Heywood, Colin. *A History of Childhood: Children and Childhood in the West from Medieval to Modern Times.* Hoboken, NJ: John Wiley & Sons, 2013.

Higson, Andrew, and Richard Maltby. *"Film Europe" and "Film America": Cinema, Commerce and Cultural Exchange, 1920–1939.* Exeter, UK: University of Exeter Press, 1999.

Hill, Daniel Delis. *As Seen in Vogue: A Century of American Fashion in Advertising.* Lubbock, TX: Texas Tech University Press, 2007.

"History as Popular Reading," *New York Times,* August 9, 1925, 16.

Huber, Werner, Martin Middeke, and Hubert Zapf. *Self-Reflexivity in Literature.* Germany: Königshausen & Neumann, 2005.

Hughes-Warrington, Marnie. *The History on Film Reader.* London: Routledge, 2009.

Iggers, Georg G. *Deutsche Geschichtswissenschaft: eine Kritik der traditionellen Geschichtsauffassung von Herder bis zur Gegenwart.* Austria: Böhlau Verlag Wien, 1997.

———. *Historiography in the Twentieth Century: From Scientific Objectivity to the Postmodern Challenge.* Middletown, CT: Wesleyan University Press, 2005.

Johnson, Mark. *The Meaning of the Body: Aesthetics of Human Understanding.* Chicago: University of Chicago Press, 2007.

Joyce, James. *Ulysses.* New York: Oxford University Press, 1998.

Jung, Uli, Walter Schatzberg, Cinémathèque municipale de Luxembourg, Clark University (Worcester Mass.), Goethe-Institut (Munich Germany), and Thomas-Mann-Bibliothek (Luxemburg). *Filmkultur zur Zeit der Weimarer Republik: Beiträge zu einer internationalen Konferenz vom 15. bis 18. Juni 1989 in Luxemburg.* Saur, 1992.

Kaes, Anton, Baer, Nicholas, and Cowan, Michael, editors. *The Promise of Cinema: German Film Theory 1907–1933.* Berkeley: University of California, Berkeley, 2016.

Kaes, Anton. *Shell Shock Cinema: Weimar Culture and the Wounds of War.* Princeton, NJ: Princeton University Press, 2009.

Kaes, Anton, Jay, Martin, and Dimendberg, Edward. *The Weimar Republic Sourcebook.* Oakland, CA: University of California Press, 1995.

Kalbus, Oskar. *Der deutsche Lehrfilm in der Wissenschaft und im Unterricht.* Berlin: C. Heymann, 1922.

Kauffmann, Stanley, and Bruce Henstell, eds. *American Film Criticism, from the Beginnings to Citizen Kane: Reviews of Significant Films at the Time They First Appeared.* 1st ed. New York: Liveright, 1972.

Kawerau, Siegfried, et al. *Synoptische Geschichtstabellen Für Die Zeit von Etwa 1500-1920 Für Den Geschichtlichen Arbeits-Unterricht Vom Ausgang Des Mittelalters Bis Zur Gegenwart.* Berlin: Schneider Verlag, 1921.

Keathley, Christian. *Cinephilia and History, or, the Wind in the Trees.* Bloomington, IN: Indiana University Press, 2006.

Kern, Stephen. *The Culture of Time and Space, 1880–1918: With a New Preface.* 2nd ed. Cambridge, MA: Harvard University Press, 2003.

Klein, Kerwin Lee. "On the Emergence of Memory in Historical Discourse." *Representations* no. 69 (January 1, 2000): 127–50.

Klein, Milton M. "Everyman His Own Historian: Carl Becker as Historiographer." *The History Teacher* 19, no. 1 (November 1, 1985): 101–9.

Knowlton, D. C. "The New History and the Photoplay." *Historical Outlook* 19, no. 2 (February 1, 1928): 70–75.

Koch, Gertrud. *Siegfried Kracauer: An Introduction.* Princeton, NJ: Princeton University Press, 2000.

Köpke, Wulf. *The Critical Reception of Alfred Döblin's Major Novels.* Rochester, NY: Camden House, 2003.

Koselleck, Reinhart, and Keith Tribe. *Futures Past: On the Semantics of Historical Time.* New York: Columbia University Press, 1985.

Kracauer, Siegfried. *From Caligari to Hitler: A Psychological History of the German Film*. Princeton, NJ: Princeton University Press, 1947.

———. *The Mass Ornament: Weimar Essays*. Cambridge, MA: Harvard University Press, 1995.

———. *Theory of Film: The Redemption of Physical Reality*. Princeton, NJ: Princeton University Press, 1960.

———. *Werke 6*.3: *Kleine Schriften zum Film 1932–61*, edited by Inka Mülder-Bach, Mirjam Wenzel, and Sabine Biebl. Frankfurt: Suhrkamp, 2004.

Krajewski, Markus. *Restlosigkeit: Weltprojekte um 1900*. Frankfurt am Main: Fischer Taschenbuch Verlag, 2006.

Kreimeier, Klaus. *The Ufa Story: A History of Germany's Greatest Film Company, 1918–1945*. Oakland, CA: University of California Press, 1999.

Kreiselmeier, Leo. *Schulkinematographie. Der Film in Schule, Jugendpflege, Verein und Heim*. Berlin: Union Deutsche Verl. Ges. o.J. 80 S. Union Deutsche Verlag Ges., 1925.

Landsberg, Alison. *Prosthetic Memory: The Transformation of American Remembrance in the Age of Mass Culture*. New York: Columbia University Press, 2004.

Landy, Marcia. *The Historical Film: History and Memory in Media*. London: Continuum International Publishing Group, 2001.

Lange, Konrad. *Das Kino in Gegenwart und Zukunft*. Enke, 1920.

Lejeune, Caroline Alice. *Cinema*. London: Alexander Maclehose, 1931.

Leslie, Esther. *Walter Benjamin*. London: Reaktion Books, 2007.

Lessing, Gotthold Ephraim. *Laokoon, Oder, Über Die Grenzen Der Malerei Und Poesie: Studienausgabe*. Reclams Universal-Bibliothek, Nr. 18865. Stuttgart: Reclam, 2012.

Liebert, Artur. "'Madame Dubarry' der Aufschwung des deutschen Films," *Der Film* 38, (1919): 46.

Lizska, James Jacob. *General Introduction to the Semiotic of Charles Sanders Peirce*. Bloomington, IN: Indiana University Press, 1996.

Lukács, György. *The Historical Novel*. London: Merlin Press, 1962.

Lulenberg, Herbert. "Festspruch zur Eröffnung des UFA-Palastes am Zoo mit dem Film Madame Dubarry," *Illustrierte Filmwoche* 39, (1919): 385.

Macintyre, Stuart, Juan Maiguashca, and Attila Pók. *The Oxford History of Historical Writing: Volume 4: 1800–1945*. New York: Oxford University Press, 2011.

Manovich, Lev. *The Language of New Media*. Cambridge, MA: MIT Press, 2001.

Marcus, Alan S. *Celluloid Blackboard: Teaching History With Film*. IAP, 2006.

Marcus, A. S., Paxton, Richard J., Meyerson, P. "'The Reality of it All,' History Students Read the Movies," *Theory and Research in Social Education* 34, no. 3 (2006): 516–52.

Marot, Helen. "The Creative and Efficiency Concepts in Education," *Dial*, April 11, 1918, 341–44.

Mast, Gerald, and Marshall Cohen. *Film Theory and Criticism; Introductory Readings*. New York: Oxford University Press, 1974.

Mattheisen, Donald J. "Filming U.S. History during the 1920s: The Chronicles of America Photoplays." *Historian* 54, no. 4 (June 1992): 627–40.

Maurer, Kathrin. *Discursive Interaction: Literary Realism and Academic Historiography in Nineteenth-Century Germany.* Synchron, 2006.

McCormick, Richard, and Alison Guenther-Pal. *German Essays on Film.* London: Continuum International Publishing Group, 2004.

———. "Sex, History, and Upward Mobility: Ernst Lubitsch's Madame Dubarry/ Passion, 1919," *German Studies Review* 33, no. 3 (October 2010): 603–17.

———. "Ernst Lubitsch & the Transnational Twenties: The Student Prince in Old Heidelberg (USA 1927), *TRANSIT* 10, no. 2 (2016): 1–10.

McCourt, John. *Roll Away the Reel World: James Joyce and Cinema.* Cork University Press, 2010.

Meindl, Dieter, and Friedrich W. Horlacher. *Mythos und Aufklärung in der amerikanischen Literatur = Myth and enlightenment in American literature. Zu Ehren von Hans-Joachim Lang.* Erlangen: Universitätsbund Erlangen-Nürnberg: Auslieferung, Universitätsbibliothek Erlangen-Nürnberg, 1985.

Merleau-Ponty, Maurice, and Talia Welsh. *Child Psychology and Pedagogy: The Sorbonne Lectures 1949–1952.* Evanston, IL: Northwestern University Press, 2010.

———. Translated by Colin Smith. *Phenomenology of Perception.* London: Routledge, 1962.

Meteling, Arno. *Monster: Zu Körperlichkeit und Medialität im modernen Horrorfilm.* Bielefeld, Germany: Transcript Verlag, 2006.

Metz, Christian. *The Imaginary Signifier: Psychoanalysis and the Cinema.* Bloomington, IN: Indiana University Press, 1982.

Mitchell, W. J. T., and Mark B. N. Hansen. *Critical Terms for Media Studies.* Chicago: University of Chicago Press, 2010.

"Mr. Wells Turns Historian," *New York Times*, November 14, 1920, 25.

Mueller, Agnes C. *German Pop Culture: How "American" Is It?.* Ann Arbor, MI: University of Michigan Press, 2004.

Münsterberg, Hugo. *The Photoplay: A Psychological Study.* New York: Appleton, 1916.

Murray, Bruce, and Christopher J. Wickham. *Framing the Past: The Historiography of German Cinema and Television.* Carbondale, IL: SIU Press, 1992.

New York Times, August 4, 1922, 21.

New York Times, July 10, 1925, 17.

New York Times, June 26, 1923, 14.

New York Times, May 5, 1921, 4.

New York Times, May 5, 1922, 34.

Nietzsche, Friedrich Wilhelm. *On The Advantage and Disadvantage of History for Life.* Indianpolis, IN: Hackett Publishing, 1980.

Oswald, Richard. "Die Aussichten des Grossen Historischen Films auf dem Weltmarkt," *Der Kinematograph* 806, (1922): 60.

Paletschek, Sylvia. *Popular Historiographies in the 19th and 20th Centuries: Cultural Meanings, Social Practices.* New York: Berghahn Books, 2011.

Pallasmaa, Juhani. "Hapticity and Time: Notes on Fragile Architecture." *Architectural Review* 207, no. 1239 (May 2000): 78–84.

Pauck, Wilhelm. *Harnack and Troeltsch*. Drew University. Drew Lectureship in Biography 1967. New York: Oxford University Press, 1968.

Paul, Gerhard. *Visual History*. Germany: Vandenhoeck & Ruprecht, 2006.

Pfitzer, Gregory M. *Popular History and the Literary Marketplace, 1840–1920*. Amherst, MA: University of Massachusetts Press, 2008.

"Philadelphia Society Attends Premiere of First National's Big Drama 'Passion,'" *Moving Picture World*, December 4, 1920, 599.

Pratt, David. "O Lubitsch, Where Wert Thou?" *Wide Angle* 13 (January 1991): 34–70.

Printy, Michael, Christopher Ocker, Peter Wallace, and Peter Starenko, eds. *Politics and Reformations: Histories and Reformations*. Leiden: Brill, 2007.

Prinzler, Hans Helmut, and Patalas, Enno. *Lubitsch*. Munich: CJ Bucher, 1984.

"Producers Busy With History's High Spots: Ripping Up Histories," *New York Times*, July 25, 1923, WF4.

"Professors Assail History by Wells," *New York Times*, May 9, 1922, 13.

Radstone, Susannah, and Bill Schwarz. *Memory: Histories, Theories, Debates*. Bronx, NY: Fordham University Press, 2010.

Ranke, Leopold von. *The Secret of World History: Selected Writings on the Art and Science of History*. Bronx, NY: Fordham University Press, 1981.

———. *The Theory and Practice of History: Edited with an Introduction by Georg G. Iggers*. Taylor & Francis, 2010.

"Rewriting History," *New York Times*, September 12, 1921, 9.

Richards, Rashna Wadia. *Cinematic Flashes: Cinephilia and Classical Hollywood*. Bloomington, IN: Indiana University Press, 2012.

Ricoeur, Paul. *Memory, History, Forgetting*. Translated by Kathleen Blamey and David Pellauer. 1st ed. Chicago: University Of Chicago Press, 2004.

Rizzolatti, Giacomo, and Corrado Sinigaglia. *Mirrors in the Brain: How Our Minds Share Actions, Emotions, and Experience*. New York: Oxford University Press, 2008.

Robinson, James Harvey. *The New History: Essays Illustrating the Modern Historical Outlook*. London: The Macmillan Company, 1912.

Rode, Franz Rudolf. "Kino und Weltpolitik," *Der Kinematograph* 784, (1922).

Rodowick, D. N. *The Virtual Life of Film*. Cambridge, MA: Harvard University Press, 2009.

Rogowski, Christian. *The Many Faces of Weimar Cinema: Rediscovering Germany's Filmic Legacy*. Rochester, NY: Camden House, 2010.

Roman, Frederick William. *The New Education in Europe: An Account of Recent Fundamental Changes in the Educational Philosophy of Great Britain, France and Germany*. 2d impression. London: New York: G. Routledge; E. P. Dutton, 1924.

Rosen, Philip. *Change Mummified: Cinema, Historicity, Theory*. Minneapolis, MN: University of Minnesota Press, 2001.

Rosenfeld, Hugo. "Music and Motion Pictures," *Annals of the American Academy of Political and Social Science*. Vol. 128 of *The Motion Picture in Its Economic and Social Aspects* (November, 1926): 58–62.

Rosenstone, Robert A. "History in Images/History in Words: Reflections on the Possibility of Really Putting History onto Film." *The American Historical Review* 93, no. 5 (December 1988): 1173–85.

———. *Visions of the Past: The Challenge of Film to Our Idea of History*. Cambridge, MA: Harvard University Press, 1995.

Rosenstone, Robert A., and Constantin Parvulescu. *A Companion to the Historical Film*. Hoboken, NJ: John Wiley & Sons, 2012.

Rusch, Gebhard, Helmut Schanze, and Gregor Schwering. *Theorien der neuen Medien: Kino, Radio, Fernsehen, Computer*. Paderborn, Germany: Wilhelm Fink Verlag, 2007.

Salmi, Hannu. "Film as Historical Narrative," *Film-Historia* 5, no. 1 (1995): 45–54.

Sältzer, Rolf, ed. *German Essays on History: Hegel, Ranke, Spengler, and Others*. 1st ed. London: Bloomsbury Academic, 1991.

Saunders, Thomas J. *Hollywood in Berlin: American Cinema and Weimar Germany*. Berkeley: University of California Press, 1994.

Scheunemann, Dietrich. *Expressionist Film: New Perspectives*. Rochester, NY: Camden House, 2006.

Schickel, Richard. *D. W. Griffith: An American Life*. Hal Leonard Corporation, 1996.

Schleier, Hans. *Die Bürgerliche Deutsche Geschichtsschreibung Der WeimarerRepublik*. Schriften Des Zentralinstituts Für Geschichte 40. Berlin: Akademie-Verlag, 1975.

Schwartz, Vanessa R. "Walter Benjamin for Historians." *The American Historical Review* 106, no. 5 (December 1, 2001): 1721–43.

"Screen: Soundless Oratory," *New York Times*, February 19, 1922, 71.

Sergeant, Philip W. *The Life of Anne Boleyn*. Whitefish, MT: Kessinger Publishing, 2005.

Shaviro, Steven. *Post Cinematic Affect*. London: John Hunt Publishing, 2010.

Silberman, Marc. *German Cinema: Texts in Context*. Detroit: Wayne State University Press, 1995.

Sobchack, Vivian. "'Surge and Splendor': A Phenomenology of the Hollywood Historical Epic." *Representations* 29 (January 1, 1990): 24–49.

———. "The Insistent Fringe: Moving Images and Historical Consciousness." *History and Theory* 36, no. 4 (December 1, 1997): 4–20.

———. *Carnal Thoughts: Embodiment and Moving Image Culture*. Oakland, CA: University of California Press, 2004.

Stephenson, Nathaniel. "The Goal of the Motion Picture in Education," *Annals of the American Academy of Political and Social Science*. Vol. 128 of *The Motion Picture in Its Economic and Social Aspects* (November 1926): 116–21.

Strauven, Wanda. *The Cinema of Attractions Reloaded*. Amsterdam: Amsterdam University Press, 2006.

"The Chronicles of America Photoplays." *The Metropolitan Museum of Art Bulletin* 20, no. 7 (July 1, 1925): 186–87.

"The Screen," *New York Times*, December 13, 1920, 21.

"The Screen," *New York Times*, February 22, 1922, 22.

"The Screen," *New York Times*, March 5, 1922, 80.

Thompson, Kristin. *Herr Lubitsch Goes to Hollywood: German and American Film after World War I.* Amsterdam: Amsterdam University Press, 2005.

Tilmans, Karin, Frank van Vree, and J. M. Winter. *Performing the Past: Memory, History, and Identity in Modern Europe.* Amsterdam: Amsterdam University Press, 2010.

Toepfer, Karl. *Empire of Ecstasy: Nudity and Movement in German Body Culture, 1910–1935.* Oakland, CA: University of California Press, 1997.

Troeltsch, Ernst. "Eine Angelsächsische Ansicht der Weltgeschichte." *Historische Zeitschrift* 126, no. 2 (1922): 271–79.

Urgiss, Julius. "Der Internationale Geschmack," *Der Kinematograph* 806 (1922): 59.

Usai, Paolo Cherchi, Lorenzo Codelli, Jan-Christopher Horak, and Associazione Le Giornate del cinema muto. *Prima di Caligari: cinema tedesco, 1895–1920.* Edizioni Biblioteca dell'immagine, 1990.

Von Moltke, Johannes. *The Curious Humanist: Siegfried Kracauer in America.* Oakland, CA: University of California Press, 2016.

Ward, Janet. *Weimar Surfaces: Urban Visual Culture in 1920s Germany.* Oakland, CA: University of California Press, 2001.

Watkins, Holly. *Metaphors of Depth in German Musical Thought: From E. T. A. Hoffmann to Arnold Schoenberg.* Cambridge: Cambridge University Press, 2011.

Weitz, Eric D. *Weimar Germany: Promise and Tragedy.* Princeton, NJ: Princeton University Press, 2009.

Wells, H. G. *The Idea of a League of Nations.* Atlantic Monthly Press, 1919.

Schacht, Roland. "Filmkrise." *Weltbühne*, December 21, 1922, 646.

White, Hayden. "Historiography and Historiophoty." *The American Historical Review* 93, no. 5 (December 1, 1988): 1193–99.

White, Hayden V. *Metahistory: The Historical Imagination in Nineteenth-Century Europe.* Baltimore, MD: Johns Hopkins University Press, 1975.

———. *The Content of the Form: Narrative Discourse and Historical Representation.* Baltimore, MD: Johns Hopkins University Press, 1990.

Williams, Linda. "Film Bodies: Gender, Genre, and Excess." *Film Quarterly* 44, no. 4 (July 1991): 2–13.

Wimmer, Andreas, and Nina Glick Schiller. "Methodological Nationalism and beyond: Nation–state Building, Migration and the Social Sciences." *Global Networks* 2, no. 4 (October 1, 2002): 301–34.

Wineburg, Samuel S. *Historical Thinking and Other Unnatural Acts: Charting the Future of Teaching the Past.* Philadelphia, PA: Temple University Press, 2001.

———. "Unnatural and Essential: The Nature of Historical Thinking," *Teaching History* 129 (December 2007): 6–11.

Youth and History: A Comparative European Survey on Historical Consciousness and Political Attitudes Among Adolescents. Hamburg: Körber-Stiftung, 1997.

Wyeth, Newell Convers. *The Ladies' Home Journal*, September 1922.

Würtenberg, Gustav. "Geschichtsunterricht und Kino," *Vergangenheit und Gegenwart* 18, no. 6 (1928): 361–66.

Zsuffa, Joseph. *Béla Balázs: The Man and the Artist.* Berkeley, CA: University of California Press, 1987.

"Zur Einführung," *Bild Archiv* 1 (1920): 1.

Index